WOULD I LIE TO YOU?

WOULD I LIE TO YOU?

PRESENTS

The 100 Most Popular Lies of All Time

Peter Holmes, Ben Caudell
and Saul Wordsworth

with interjections from

Rob Brydon, Lee Mack
& David Mitchell

FABER & FABER

First published in 2015
by Faber & Faber Limited
74–77 Great Russell Street
London WC1B 3DA

Typeset by Faber & Faber Ltd
Printed in the UK by CPI Group (UK) Ltd, Croydon, CRO 4YY

A CIP record for this book
is available from the British Library

ISBN 978–0–571–32516–0 (hardback)
ISBN 978–0–571–32722–5 (export)

2 4 6 8 10 9 7 5 3 1

Introduction

As the creator and executive producer of *Would I Lie To You?* I am rarely, if ever, asked to describe the moment of inspiration that led me to conceive the two-time BAFTA-losing show. I once tried talking to a stranger on the underground about it, but he shooed me away with a copy of the *Metro* and changed train at the next stop. I contacted my old school and offered to give a talk, but the headmaster never returned my calls. My dry cleaner turns the sign to 'closed' whenever I pass; my neighbours cross the street. Cats leap from walls when they see me approach; trees wither and die. I sense that I am getting a reputation as something of a bore, my Twitter follower begs to differ. Thank you @spambotfromhastings for your continued support.

Well, here at last is my opportunity to tell the world how I gave birth to *Would I Lie To You?* Settle in for possibly the longest anecdote in showbiz.

My story begins in East Grinstead when I fell off a ladder as a boy . . .

. . . OK, change of plan. After lengthy discussion with my publisher, Faber & Faber, during which one man fell asleep and another resigned, I have reluctantly agreed to save this story for another time. I do so with a heavy heart and no choice in the matter. Instead, I will simply introduce the book that you are holding in your hand, very possibly in a charity shop.

Would I Lie To You Presents The 100* Most Popular Lies of All Time is the product of several days' work. If you've ever been lied to, or told a lie yourself, there's every chance that lie will be humorously scrutinised somewhere in this book. It's a book to dip into, a book to gift a friend, a book to file somewhere between your unread Dostoevsky and your well-thumbed Roddy Doyle.

Amongst the pages, you'll also find the wit and wisdom of the show's stars, Rob Brydon, Lee Mack and David Mitchell, who were obliged by hastily signed contracts to discuss many of the lies contained within. These discussions took place in a poorly ventilated room the morning after our most recent BAFTA defeat, but still their unwavering professionalism and illuminating insight leaps from the page.

I began by asking each of them to introduce this book in their own inimitable way, and I now hand you over to Rob Brydon who was brave enough to go first.

If you have read this far, you may as well read on. It can only get better.

Peter Holmes, executive producer,
Would I Lie To You?

Introduction from Rob Brydon

Dear reader, I am hopeful that this introduction will help me to reach 50 per cent of the word-count I'm contractually obliged to deliver to Faber & Faber as part of a two-book deal.

Fans of *Would I Lie To You?* will be delighted at the compendium of lies, half-truths and deceits contained herein. You don't need me to tell you that this book is the result of a lot of work, a lot of sweat and . . . something like that, blah, blah, blah, and so on.

Please enjoy this book, whether you're dipping in, or cramming for an exam. Er . . . Da-di-da-di-da-di-da-di-da.

David:

How far down the page is he now?

Rob:

You get the idea, transcribe that and we're on our way. So that's my bit, David, it's your turn.

David:

But you've stolen the idea of not giving a damn! All right, I'll give it a go.

Introduction from David Mitchell

Thank you for buying this book. Although it is a shame, perhaps, that at this festive time of year, you've chosen a product based entirely on falsity, and an increasingly discredited populist medium. Nevertheless . . .

Lee:
Is one more word.

David:
Nevertheless, from my point of view, you seeking out some merchandise can only enhance the brand of what I hope will continue to be a successful television programme. Personally, I'm more excited about the lunch box.

Don't lie if it causes hurt, but do lie if it can get you out of a hole; and I mean that literally and metaphorically.

Merry Christmas, if indeed it is Christmas, which it's perfectly possible it isn't.

Lee, it's your turn.

Introduction from Lee Mack

THIS BOOK BELONGS TO

_____

AGE _____

LIE # 1

" I am away for two weeks with NO access to email. "

As lies go, this is one we have all told and secretly all respect. It's also a lie we're so committed to that we engage a machine to tell it for us. The night before we leave the office for a much-needed break we open our Out of Office Assistants and type the lie: 'I am away for two weeks with no access to email.' There, it must be true. It says so in black and white, and it's not in Comic Sans.

Those less confident will opt for the 'I'm away for two weeks with *limited* access to email' and those who are afraid of being caught out and not very good at lying will type something like: 'I'm away for two weeks and Derek, the man who owns the cottage we are staying in, said the wi-fi is pretty patchy and often cuts out if any horses come too close to the kitchen door, so I probably won't be able to check email that much, if at all, so please wait until I'm back unless it's urgent, in which case try Martin who sits at the desk near me (he's got red hair and is often eating cereal).'

The sad fact of the modern world is that we shouldn't have to tell this lie at all. What's wrong with just going on

1

holiday? That's what people used to do. In a pre-digital age you could clock off on a Friday evening and completely forget about work for two weeks. You could happily sit on the beach or wander around museums nursing a pint without fear of anybody from the office bothering you. But then things got all 'connected' and mobile phones happened and suddenly you found yourself stood in the queue for the zoo wiping jam off a toddler's face while conference-calling Australia. So ultimately, you're forced to lie.

We all know that internet access can be a bit slow in places, sometimes it even cuts out, but to have *no* access whatsoever is almost impossible in this Google-sponsored world. What you're really saying is: 'I'm on holiday and I'm not planning to look at emails and I don't want to be bothered by you, and yes, I know there is a hillock round the back of the cottage where it's possible to stand on an old barrel and get a bit of signal but I don't want to do that, and yes, I do remember last August when John used to take that pedalo out every morning to that spot opposite the church in the old town where he could tap into the occasional passing tanker's wi-fi and keep up to date with the latest developments in the office but that's John and he's been deeply depressed since his wife left him and I don't want my life to turn out like his.'

And that's OK. Most of us are happy to read your Out of Office message and pretend that we believe it, because we know that we'll be writing exactly the same thing when it's our turn to go on holiday. The ones that find it insulting are office bores with no life outside of the workplace, pale skin and high blood pressure. They think 'work' in itself is important and that is their great mistake.

Forget them and hurl your laptop into the sea. They are for the early grave and the Out of Office tombstone.

LIE # 2

"My alcohol intake is about eleven units a week."

When a doctor asks you how many units of alcohol you drink per week they are not expecting a straight answer. Every time they ask the question they know that the patient is going to say a figure less than the actual amount they consume. The challenge for the patient is to say a figure that seems plausible; the challenge for the doctor is to look like they actually believe it.

The conversation usually goes something like this.

Doctor:
How many units of alcohol would you say you drink per week?

Patient [*stalling for time*]:
Have you read *The Wasp Factory*?

Doctor:
There's no need to take off your trousers.

Patient [*pulling trousers back up*]:
Sorry, I thought you asked to look at my knee.

Once this pantomime is out of the way he asks you again and you start to make the mental calculations. You know that men are advised to drink no more than twenty-one units per week, and for the purposes of this book entry I am assuming, dear reader, that you are a man. (But not just any old man, a feminist man. A man who follows Caitlin Moran on Twitter and has a poster of Pussy Riot on his wall.)

Patient:
Well I doubt I drink as much as they advise. I rarely reach the twenty-one units a week.

Doctor:
That's not a target, that's a limit.

Patient:
And a very generous one at that, if you ask me!

Doctor:
So how many would you say?

Now your brain goes into calculation mode. You didn't have a drink last night at all, so theoretically if the week began last night you could say you drank none. But, realistically, you did drink the night before that, and the one before that, so that probably counts. And the night before that was Friday when you really let your hair down and ended up in a karaoke bar singing that Crash Test Dummies song at your own reflection. Then there was Thursday when you had a fairly boozy lunch and on Wednesday you won the pub quiz, even though you were completely drunk. That was mainly because Debbie was there, and she is so clever. What *does* she see in Steve? Tuesday was a quiet one – just a couple of lagers in front of the football and on Monday you only finished off Sunday's wine. So all in all, that's what, about ten units?

Patient:
Remind me, how much is a unit of alcohol?

Doctor:
A pint of strong lager is about three units, the same for a large glass of wine.

You think back to the pub quiz night, and how you took your shirt off as you collected your prize, and how later that night Steve asked you to get out of Debbie's front garden. Apparently they were trying to sleep.

Patient:
Then I'd say my alcohol intake is about eleven units a week. Sometimes less, sometimes a touch more, but well, there's no point in lying to you. Let's say eleven.

Brilliant, you think. The imperfectness of the number eleven, the flattery of his position, the acknowledgement that *other* people in this situation might lie. If you weren't at the doctor's you'd have a glass of wine to celebrate, but instead you just smile and say your goodbyes. Alone in his room the doctor closes your file and sighs. It's only two thirty and he's here until six. He takes a bottle from the filing cabinet, has a nip, and makes a mental note to buy some mints on the way home.

Lies to watch out for from ... **Plumbers**

LIE # **3**

"I'll need to get a part."

Imagine you are a plumber. You have been to plumbing school and passed your plumbing exams. You have bought a van and painted the name of your plumbing business on the side*. You have advertised your business on local shop windows and paid for an advert in the local paper. You have asked your neighbour's thirteen-year-old son to design you a website because he is good with computers. (He's nearly done it, but had to stop for karate

---

* To decide the name of your plumbing business you need to consider all the options. They are as follows.

Option 1: Use your first name only, e.g. 'Mark's Plumbing'. Unless you have a really interesting first name, something like D'Artagnan, this is not a good option. It sounds a bit weak and unmemorable.

Option 2: Use your surname, e.g. 'Higson's Plumbing'. This is a better option and carries a bit more weight. If you are planning to trap your son into becoming a plumber you can add the 'and son' to the side of the van now, though that may feel like a noose around his neck for the entirety of his childhood. Adding 'and daughter' makes you sound progressive and interesting. This will play well with the ABC1 clients. Even if you don't have a daughter this is probably worth doing. In a crowded marketplace you will stand out.

Remember, some surnames are not good names for plumbers. Leak, Drip, Bodge or Ripoff spring to mind.

Option 3: Give your business a catchy name, usually based around a pun. Floody Marvellous, Cistern Addicts, It's Draining Men will all look good on your van and will entertain other motorists.

practice; it should be ready by Tuesday.) The phone rings. You answer it. The person on the other end is freezing cold and wants you to come and fix their boiler. Your first job! You've made it! You are a plumber!

You read the *Daily Mirror* for a bit and drink a chocolate milk, then hop into your van and drive to the freezing cold house. The person inside is pleased to see you. They get you to feel the ice-cold radiators and take you to the boiler cupboard. You recognise the make and model from plumbing school. There are only really two types of boiler and this is one of them. The pilot light is out and it won't restart. You remove the cover from the boiler and see that a valve needs replacing. As this is your first day as a plumber you don't have this valve on your van, so you tell the freezing cold person that you'll need to go and get it from a shop. They don't really care; they just want it fixed. So you drive to a plumbers' merchants, pick up the part and bring it back to the house. You fix the boiler and check that the heating is now working. You charge them for two hours' labour plus the cost of the valve. If you'd had the part on the van it would only have been an hour's labour, but they are warm now so everything is all right. They pay you and you drive home in your van. Your plumber's van. After all, you are now a plumber.

The next morning, your phone rings again. Somebody is freezing cold and needs your help. You eat a bag of Monster Munch and drive to their house. They show you to the boiler, it's the same make and model as the one you fixed yesterday. You open it up and see that the same valve needs replacing. As this is only your second day of being a plumber you don't have the valve on your van so you tell the shivering person you'll need to go and get a part. You drive back to the plumbers' merchants you went to yesterday and buy another valve. You drive back to the house, fix the boiler, take the payment and get back in your van. You're about to drive home when your phone rings. A cold person needs your help to fix their boiler. Two jobs in one day! Your reputation as a plumber is growing. You eat some sausage and chips in the van then drive to the chilly house.

The owner answers the door in a thick jumper and scarf. They show you their boiler. It's just like the two you've already fixed. You open it up and see that the valve needs replacing. As this is still only your second day of being a plumber you don't have a new valve on the van so you tell them you'll need to go and get a part. You drive to the plumbers' merchants and pick up another valve. As you take it to the counter you are struck by an incredible thought. *What if I bought a whole box of these valves?* you think. *I wouldn't need to keep coming back here every day. I could fix the boilers in half the time and save money on petrol.*

You buy a box of valves, and while you are there you pick up other parts you anticipate might need replacing in the course of your work. You load them into your van, drive back to the igloo and fix the boiler. The cold person pays you for the part and the labour and you drive home eating some ham.

That evening the boy from next door shows you the website he's been working on. It looks pretty good but he's spelled 'plumber' wrong. He's written 'plumer'. Nobody needs a 'plumer'. He tells you he'll fix it but he's got to go to judo now. It should be done by Friday.

The next morning, your phone rings. A cold person wants you to fix their boiler. You eat a bun and drink a bottle of Lucozade. You drive to their house and look at the boiler. It's just like all the other boilers you've fixed and it needs a new valve. You've got about twenty of them on the van. You bought them yesterday, anticipating this very problem. You look at your watch. This job is going to be done very quickly, about half the time of all the others. And that's when you realise the fault with your new way of working. Half the time is half the money. Who in their right mind works for half the money when freezing cold people are happy to pay double just to get warm? You replace the boiler cover and think about this for a while. You head downstairs and find the owner. They are sat on the sofa wearing a duffel coat and a balaclava. Their breath clings to the air like puffs of fog, their fingers are blue. They ask you if you know what the problem is. You tell them you do, and that it's pretty easy to fix, and then for the first time in your new career you tell the big fat lie, 'I'll need to get a part.'

Congratulations! You really are a plumber! You told the great plumber lie!

You climb into your van and drive about four streets away. You park up at the side of the road and eat some cheese. You listen to Talk Radio. While sat there you notice another plumber's van parked up on the other side of the road, and another just in front of that. Another one swings into view in your rear-view mirror and parks up behind you. Another one parks behind that and then another and another. The street is now full of plumbers who have gone to get a part. You swap knowing looks and share Pringles together. Someone gets a football and starts a plumbers' kick about; someone grabs a ukulele and sings a plumbers' song. You link arms, all plumbers together, and join them in a chorus, singing at the top of your voice, 'We've gone to get a part, we've gone to get a part, we won't be back for over an hour, we've gone to get a part!'

An hour passes and an alarm sounds on a plumber's phone. Legions of bald men scurry to their vans and climb into their cabs. The street is filled with the sound of Ford Transit doors slamming and engines revving. You inch into the traffic and head for the broken boiler. You replace the valve and get the heating pumping around the house. The customer removes their balaclava and asks you for the bill. You check your watch and note the time. You explain that strictly speaking you are now into the third hour, but you'll knock the last ten minutes off and call it two. You take their money and say your good-byes. They thank you for being so good about the time.

Back in your cab you sit in silence for a moment fingering the thickness of your wallet. Today, for the very first time, you peeked behind the curtain and it felt almost spiritual. You eat a king-size Mars and drink two litres of Coke. It feels good to be alive. Your phone rings. A cold person wants you to come and fix their boiler. You tell them you're sure you can fix it by the end of the day, but you might just need to go and get a part.

LIE # **4**

x (*Kiss*)

Did you really mean to sign off with an 'x' when you texted your meter reading to Southern Water?

Did you really mean to give the man from Foxtons a 'x' at the end of the email saying you were no longer looking for flats in the Petts Wood area?

Did you really mean to send a text to the mechanic asking what time you can pick your car up, and end it with a 'x'?

Do you actually want to kiss the computer at Southern Water? On the lips? And what about the man from Foxtons? Are you actually saying you would kiss him ON THE LIPS if you met him? No. The mechanic though, he is quite cute. So maybe.

There was an age when the only time you would sign off a message with a 'x' was to a close loved one. There was good reason for that: because 'x' means 'kiss'.

So why did we start sending kisses to our bosses, our workmates and that bloke from the Red Lion? Do we want to kiss them? No. So why are we saying we feel so well disposed towards them that we would actually like to kiss them?

It was the text message that changed the way people behaved. Suddenly a message that just said 'See you in the pub at 8' looked a little naked if it didn't have some sort of punctuation mark on the end. A smiley emoticon soon became a bit naff if you were over twelve. Sometimes an exclamation mark could fill the void! Or a question mark? But if the message didn't require them, then you'd just go for a 'x'.

And then everyone was getting them: people you'd just met, hairdressers, Camden Council. They all got kisses. And that meant that one 'x' was no longer enough. Pretty soon you were having to decide if a Polish odd-job man whose name you weren't sure of deserved two or three 'x's – and that's someone whose number you had recorded in your phone as 'Pavel??? Polish Man'.

But you might say, this isn't a lie. Everyone knows you don't actually want to kiss them. It's just a sign-off, a piece of punctuation, a formality. It's the same as ending a letter with 'yours sincerely' – no one is actually being sincere; it's just how you end things.

The lying comes when you decide to remove the 'x' from the text to a loved one, when you feel that they are somehow in your bad books. You know they'll notice that there's no kiss, and that's as good as saying you currently care for them less than someone from esure or Trailfinders. You want them to notice you're cross, and you know that missing off the 'x' will leave them in no doubt. You're even hinting that maybe that's it.

You never want to kiss them again, you're so furious.

But the truth is, you're lying, because you know there's no one in the world that could replace them.

Yours sincerely,

x

It's very common on text and email to sign off with an x for a kiss. Do you worry about who you are kissing?

Lee:
I don't worry at all because I have a blanket ban on it.

Rob:
I have a blanket insistence on it. I kiss people I barely know and I attribute that to my enduring theatricality.

Lee:
If it takes up too much space to put 'enduring theatricality' just put 'falseness'.

Rob:
Or if you're really pushed, just put 'berk'.

Lee:
Yes.

David:

That works.

Lee:

My basic rule is this: don't put a kiss unless you would kiss them on the lips.

David:

I would accept that logic and if I was a more demonstrative person I think I would put a kiss if I would kiss that person on the cheek, but I don't even do that.

Lee:

Well, a kiss on the cheek counts for nothing nowadays because everyone's kissing everyone and everyone is hugging everyone.

David:

Except in the moment where you decide OK, I'm going to go in for the kiss and then, oh no, suddenly kissing's been banned; suddenly I'm disgusting!

And do you go for one or two kisses?

David:

I like to be awkward, so whatever they're thinking they don't do, I'll go for that. I'm hoping for a big nose bump.

Rob:

I've become a double kisser, but I'd like to go back to just giving one.

Lee:

Why can't we just go back to being repressed? That was great.

David:

Yes, what this country needs is a major bacterial infection that will stop all this unnecessary touching.

Lee:

Good idea.

David:

I only put kisses on texts and emails to my wife and that's it.

Rob:

Well that's as it should be. But do you know what has really helped in all this? The emoji. I've adopted them quite recently. In fact I used one this morning with a little wink for one of my kids.

Lee:

My rules are: I will not wink at anyone in a text unless I would wink at them face to face.

Rob:

Well, I like them because I do think that they can convey exactly what you want to convey. Sometimes with a little embarrassed face, sometimes with a proud face. I think they are rather nice and rather helpful.

18

David:

Yes, because everyone's been struggling to express human emotion using just the English language for hundreds of years and now all that poetry is thankfully over because we can just use an emoji that sums us up. So, bad luck, Shakespeare, now we can use it all as loo roll.

Rob:

But think what he could have accomplished had he had access to emojis. 'Shall I compare thee to a summer's day?' would have been a question mark followed by a lovely picture of some beautiful idyll . . .

David:

Yes, the subtlety of Shakespeare's emojis would make the Mona Lisa look like a big grinning bird.

LIE # 5

" We really *must* go for a drink sometime. "

It's an old friend. It's someone from school. It's someone you went to college with. It's a person from a company your company used to work with. It's an old flame. It's a friend of a friend.

It's nice to see them when you bump into them in the street or in Marks & Spencer's food hall or at a funeral or at a party at a friend of a friend's house or on a train, as long as you aren't heading in the same direction. 'Where are you heading? . . . Oh, I'm going to a slightly different place by a slightly different route.'

You actually enjoy talking to them, they seem all right really. Nice to chat to for a bit. Not for ages – a chat with an end in sight. And then, just as you are getting off the train or packing your bags at the tills, one of you absent-mindedly utters the words: 'We must go for a drink sometime.'

And the other one answers, 'Yes, that would be nice.'

At this particular point, neither party is lying. Yes it would be nice to go for a drink at some point. That doesn't sound awful. As long as it never actually happens.

Because both of you know that the phrase 'We must go for a drink sometime' doesn't actually mean you want to go for a drink with someone. It just means 'I like you enough to say that I'd like to go for a drink with you that never actually happens.' Everyone knows that, don't they?

That's the beauty of the word 'sometime'. It sounds like it should have the word 'soon' on the end, so that it feels slightly urgent, but it could actually mean 'at the end of time and space'.

And most of the time it doesn't happen. Which is great. No one says anything else about it. Both parties happy in the knowledge that they would theoretically like to give up a small portion of an evening to chew the fat, as long as it never actually happens in reality. It's just enough to know that that is the level of ambition you have for this particular relationship – a friendly non-relationship. And if you see each other again, at the doctors or on a bus or at a wedding or in a National Trust property car park, then you'll exchange pleasantries and say, 'We must go for that drink sometime.'

Because, once you've had the time to think about it, if you ever actually went for a drink with them, you have no idea what you would talk about. It would be awful. It would be boring. They would be boring. What a waste of an evening you could be doing nothing in.

But occasionally one of you gets the wrong end of the stick. One of you actually forgets that neither of you actually wants to go for a drink with the other person. One of you – normally not you, normally the other person obviously – starts to *actually* try to make arrangements for it to *actually* happen.

Whether this is because they believe your relationship is more intense than it actually is, or because they are somehow calling your bluff, doesn't matter, because there's no way of telling the two apart. You get an email headed 'Drink?' and saying something along the lines of: 'Thought I would get the ball rolling for this drink thing. How you fixed the week after the week after next?'

Of course, you're busy the week after the week after next. But you say you might be free the week after the week after the week after next. They'll probably never even get back to you. But they do. A date is arranged. The week *after* the week after the week after next. Place to be confirmed nearer the time. It's OK, because you know the meeting *will never actually happen.*

The first time, the meeting is cancelled because something unavoidable comes up a few days before. You feel compelled to rearrange the date, the week after the week after the week after next, to keep up the dance.

Don't worry, it will *never actually happen.*

And how true that is. Because this second arrangement also falls through a few days before it is meant to happen. This time they cancel. They'll get back to you with a new date.

Maybe they have worked out that you both don't really want to meet, and it will *never actually happen.*

But then, they do start to arrange another date. And you fix another date. The week *after* the week after the week after the week after next.

Don't worry, it will *never actually happen.*

But then, in the days before the date in question, nothing seems to prevent the meeting happening. Nothing comes up, not at your end, not at theirs.

On the day itself, you even get as far as exchanging emails arranging a place and time.

The day ticks on. They're going to cancel. They have to cancel. Why haven't they cancelled?

Only a couple of hours to go. You have to do something. Otherwise this drink might actually happen.

You are forced into desperate measures. You start to text them: 'Really sorry but . . .' and then another round of LYING begins.

At this late stage you have to make your lie so stunning, so unexpected, so weird, that the other person is in no doubt that you are lying through your teeth.

And they know why you are doing it:

This drink must *never actually happen.*

LIE # 6

" I have read the terms and conditions. "

In the same way that no one has ever read *A Brief History of Time* or *One Direction: Our Band, Our Story*, no one has ever read the 'terms and conditions' of a website or programme.

And why would they? They are long, boring and make no sense. The terms and conditions for Apple's iTunes service come in at around 20,000 words, about the length of a short novella by Will Self and only slightly more interesting to read.

At the fastest adult reading speed of 300 words a minute it would take almost an hour to read all of these terms and conditions, let alone work out if you agree with all of them. Does anyone have time to read that when all they really want to do is download a copy of 'Boom Shack-A-Lak' by Apache Indian, the best song in the world?

> 'Hey, this is a great party! The only thing that could improve it, and your chances of getting off with me, is if we could dance to "Boom Shack-A-Lak" by Apache Indian, the best song in the word. Have you got it?'

'No, but I'll install Apple iTunes and download it!'

'Great. I'm really looking forward to dancing to it straightaway. I get sexy when I dance. But only to that particular song.'

'Oh hold on, I have to read 15,000 words of terms and conditions before we can dance to "Boom Shack-A-Lak" by Apache Indian.'

'I'm getting bored. I think I might go home now.'

'But I need to read these before I can download it.'

'Why don't you just lie and say you've read them?'

'OK. Now I can download it.'

'I'm going.'

'I thought you would stay if I got that song?'

'You lied about the terms and conditions. I don't need another liar in my life. I had enough of that with my last boyfriend.'

This terms and conditions lie is a classic case, where both parties know that a lie is being told, but it is in both their interests to maintain the lie. You get the software or service you want straightaway, and the company, knowing you haven't really read the terms and conditions, has got you to effectively agree to a contract that may contain anything.

Who knows what's in these T&Cs? You might be signing up to have a kidney removed, or fight for the Syrian rebels, or become part of a medical trial for an Ebola vaccine. You might have agreed that masked men can enter your house at midnight and drain your testicles of sperm with a massive pipette. You might have agreed that you will be cooked and eaten by Michael Gove. The truth is, you just don't know. None of us do. And at any point – as the result of blindly agreeing to the terms and conditions of Angry Birds Rio – we might be dragged away to have a live colonoscopy on Channel 5.

Think of that next time you click on 'I have read the terms and conditions'.

Exercises

1. Read some terms and conditions. Try not to kill yourself at the 342nd paragraph. You're only halfway through.

2. Write your own terms and conditions and send them to Apple. See if you get a response.

LIE # 7

" You don't look your age. "

People are obsessed with age. Kids want to be older, everyone else wants to be younger, except Moira Stuart who is happy the way things are. But unless you've been asleep since the beginning of time you'll know that this is an area of great sensitivity, greater even than Liverpool or the perineum.

Let's say you're at work (I hope you've got a job). There's a group of you chatting out the back by the bins. Amongst you is a woman who you imagine to be in her early fifties. Her face looks lived in, maybe by up to a hundred squirrels, all past their prime.

'Go on, guess my age,' she says.
　'Fifteen,' you say.
　'I'm twenty-nine,' comes her response.
　'I can't believe you're twenty-nine!' you tell her.
　'Thank you, I love you,' she says.

You dodged a bullet. Had you responded honestly a terrible silence would have ensued, followed by a swift punch to the solar plexus. But you didn't. Well done. You're a lot brighter than you look.

Telling someone they don't look their age is the surest form of flattery, more flattering even than offering to pay them for a kiss. Youth is where it's at and we can't get enough of it.

At some point we have all underestimated someone's age and as a result nearly been murdered. Thus we learnt lessons: never drop our guard, never assume and never *ever* offer an honest appraisal. There are humans at large who look so prematurely aged it is a risk, if prompted, to estimate much beyond the age of ten.

If you are concerned that *you* look your age there are a number of options available to you. These comprise not drinking, staying out of the sun, sucking a dummy, hanging out with people over a hundred, and undergoing plastic surgery. Surgical options include hair implants, Botox and ear shortening. The truth about plastic surgery is it doesn't make you look young, only odd and bulgy. The one sure-fire way to stay young is to die that way.

Why are we so offended if someone misjudges our age? Is youth so important? Didn't we all enjoy *Cocoon*? What about wisdom, integrity, judgement, experience and nasal hair with its own dandruff? Surely such qualities are as appealing as radiant beauty, extreme sexiness and a pert bottom.

The key may be gender. Where age allegedly makes men windswept and interesting, we are led to believe for women it does the opposite. Thus there is a chance – *only a chance mind* – that the woman will take less kindly to an injudicious age guestimation. But what do I know? (I thought Joan Collins was twenty-six.)

If you're looking for advice, go low or stay out of it. A game of 'guess my age' can only end badly, with the other person in floods of tears/admitting they are 106/ explaining they've recently moved into an old people's home where the staff don't cut the bananas up properly. And God knows, that can be frustrating, especially when you get to my age. How old am I? How old do I *look*?

LIE # 8

" This is a thought good enough to tweet. "

Is it though? Are you sure? This thought that you've had – is it really worth tweeting?

It's not like everything you say has to be so amazing that it's going to break the internet, but take another look at the thought you've just had, that you're about to tweet. Is it really worth it?

I know it's not much effort, just tapping away at pretend keys on the screen of your phone. It's not like a thought you would ever, say, write by hand with a pen and ink like all those old-fashioned clever writers. You'd never bother with committing this thought to actual paper; but with a few clicks you will happily send it to the world.

But that's what Twitter's for, you say, for sending clever, informative, revealing, funny things to the world. Why should Twitter be dominated by funny, clever, interesting people like Alain de Botton and Gary Lineker?

But have another look at your tweet before you click send. Is it funny? Is it informative? Is it revealing? Is it relevant? Does it have an insight into the human condition?

Or is it actually just another boring string of 140 characters that's going to clog up the internet? A thought so tediously inane that you wouldn't actually go to all the bother of opening your lips and making the shapes of the sounds of the words in order to say it out loud.

Maybe it's actually worse than that. Is it actually a thought that is bullying? Unkind? Rude? Racist? Is it a thought that you would never want anyone to know you had? A thought you would only tweet because you are hiding behind the anonymity of your username?

Before sending any tweet you should first consider whether it's worth saying to the person stood next to you at the bus stop – never mind the world. Then repeat this mental process with the person next to them, and the person next to them. Three yeses and you can feel free to tweet away. Anything less, and you should save yourself the bother and keep your thought to yourself. #justsayin

LIE # 9

Butler lies

In 2010, Cornell University professors Jeff Hancock and Jeremy Birnholtz identified a new type of lie, ushered into being by the electronic age: lies told when we simply don't want to continue a text or email conversation with someone any longer. Lies like:

> My battery's low.

> Got to go, someone at the door.

> I'm going into a tunnel.

> Better go, my mum is calling.

> I didn't get your text. Oh, it just came through. Weird.

> Sorry, I'd better go and finish my essay on text lies for Professors Hancock and Birnholtz.

They dubbed these untruths 'butler lies' – as a nod to days gone by when a butler would be instructed by his master to enter a room after five minutes to bring an unwanted conversation to an end by saying that dinner is served, or that there's a body in the library.

Quite why the professors of Cornell University were researching lies in text messages and not say, curing cancer, or trying to get off with their students at a nineties disco, is unknown, but their research revealed that 10 per cent of all text messages contain lies, and one-fifth of those are butler lies.

At least, that's what they texted their boss.

LIE # 10

"Wow, your new tattoo looks really . . . interesting!"

Tattoos used to be the preserve of sailors and criminals, but nowadays every Tom, Dick and Sally likes to have a flesh doodle. For some reason, people have decided that plain old skin is boring. Wrinkles, hairs, nipples and moles just aren't enough. Bodies need brightening with the blue-black ink of a jabbing needle. They're so ubiquitous, the police now consider the absence of a tattoo a distinguishing mark in a wanted man. So when a colleague starts unbuttoning his shirt or loosening his trousers to show you what he had done at the weekend you better get ready to tell the great tattoo lie.

'Wow, your new tattoo looks really interesting!' translates as: 'I don't know why you are showing me a picture of Frank Lampard's face on your bum, but it looks terrible and sore and actually now that I can see it more clearly I think it looks like Huw Edwards.'

It's easy to tell a friend you don't like their new hat because you know they can take it off, but a tattoo's for life, not just a stag do. Add to that permanence the indignity they'll have gone through getting inked and it's best to stick with the great tattoo lie. Nobody wants to hear the truth when they've spent the afternoon in a seafront parlour, bent double, trousers down, while a man with holes for earlobes and a chopstick through his nose squirts paint through the teeth of a red-hot needle into their arse. So just nod, smile and damn the self-abuse with faint praise.

Having told the lie you can continue to avoid speaking the truth by making other bland observations. Things like 'That must have taken a while', 'I bet that hurt' and 'Isn't it dusty in here?'

On rare occasions you may be confronted by something so beautiful you don't need to tell the lie. But as a rule of thumb, if the tattoo features: Celtic or Chinese symbols; loved-ones' names; ribbons; bows; stars; love hearts; anchors; a playing card; cigarettes; motorbikes; a snake; a ladder; a picture of Christ; a middle finger; a flag; Che Guevara; someone from Westlife; rude words; a dog; Coldplay lyrics; R2-D2; some oblique reference to *Breaking Bad*; biscuits; James May; a hen; Rudyard Kipling; a prune; Lee Dixon; the *Coronation Street* cat; Sebastian Coe; some Marmite; a map of Gravesend; Wicked Willie; the logo for *A Question of Sport*; Denholm Elliott; a frog drinking beer; baked beans; Zorro; Fred Basset; some bloke you took a shine to from *Bargain Hunt*; or the operating instructions for a combi boiler – you best grit your teeth, take a deep breath and tell them it looks, well . . . interesting!

Do any of you have a tattoo?

Lee:

I'd love to have a tattoo. I keep saying I'm going to have one but I just haven't got round to it yet.

Rob:

Why do you want one?

Lee:

I like painting, I like skin, I like needles.

David:

Does it remind you of your heroin days?

Lee:

I would have one somewhere that you couldn't see it, but you know if you wanted to impress a young biker girl it would come in handy. 'I know I look like a middle-aged man, love, but did you know I've got a rose on my arse?'

David:

Cheryl Cole has a huge rose on her arse doesn't she?

Lee:

When did she show you that?

David:

Ah, we're very close. No, she showed the newspapers. She showed all the newspapers a picture of her huge rose-on-arse tattoo.

Rob:

Surely, the whole thing is: how does anyone know that they are going to like their tattoo for ever?

Lee:

Well, I'd say the same about having children; you just have to jump in at the deep end.

Rob:

But you can have *them* removed with lasers, can't you.

Lee:

Ha!

David:

The key to the tattoo's appeal is that very attitude – that it's is an unwise and long-term solution to a short-term feeling. It's like with smoking, the fact that it's bad for you is part of its appeal now. It didn't used to be when everyone smoked, but now it's a sign of rebellion. It's a sign that you're embracing your own mortality in a mature way and, similarly, to have a tattoo is a sign. You're saying, 'Yeah, forget the future, I never want to be an accountant so I'll have a spider on my face.'

LIE # 11

" Honestly, he's fine. I love dogs. "

Getting molested by somebody else's dog is a thoroughly unpleasant experience, but one that all too often we seem happy to take on the chin, the face, the neck and the groin. Picture the scene: you've popped round somebody's house for one of the many reasons you might pop round somebody's house (to borrow some sugar, to return a travel plug, to discuss the pros and cons of laser eye surgery) and on knocking at the door you hear a commotion in the hall. It sounds like somebody has upturned a sack of rubber hammers and opened a can of woofs. The noise gets nearer with added scratches and whimpers and the letterbox starts thwacking open and shut as if possessed by a poltergeist postman. Above this din, a human voice calls out in an attempt to instil calm, then the front door opens just a slant and your friend stands there, one hand behind their back, attempting to suppress the surge of what seems like a demented barrel of fur. They beckon you to squeeze past them into the hall, and with one hand on the collar of the hound, usher you into the living room and shut the door. Alone, you catch your breath and look about the room. Photos of your friend and the beast are everywhere. They appear to be whispering together in the hallway. The door opens, and then six legs shuffle in and momentarily settle.

Your friend apologises for the welcome and you get on with the business of whatever it was you popped round for (to ask them if they liked Malta, to borrow a *Goonies* DVD, to show them your new teeth), but you can never properly relax because the thing from the hall is staring at you from under a chair and slobbering at the prospect of eating your head. Your friend senses your nervousness and offers words of reassurance. They tell you he's just a big softie who wouldn't hurt a fly. If the beast makes the slightest flicker of movement they shout his name (Spartan! Chopper! Thor!) and restrain him by grabbing the collar at the back of his neck. You do your very best to look calm and continue with the business for which you called round (to lend them a whisk, to discuss local schools, to tell them that Dom Littlewood has started following you on Twitter), but inside your nerves jangle and your palms sweat.

At some point in the conversation you unwittingly say the dog's trigger word and the afternoon takes a turn. In less than a second the thing is on your lap, his front paws pinning you to your chair while his thickening member thwacks you about the ribs. He slobbers a foamy howl across your mouth and peels back your eyelids with one sweep of his fetid, lolling tongue. He tears at your thighs with his rock-hard claws and furiously slides his glistening bum hole across your open mouth. He licks your teeth and belches in your face with enough might to turn one eyeball inside out. He kicks your jaw with the force of a dawn raid and howls a howl so deep and primitive it sounds like the death of the universe. You are helpless to respond and completely lose the thread of what you were talking about (*Poldark*? IVF? The best way to make jam?). And then he's gone.

Somehow your friend has taken control of this monster and forced him back beneath a chair. He lies on his belly, his chest heaving on the floorboards, offering you a look of complete contempt. Your friend apologises and says he's never normally like this; it's just that he's excited to see you. And that's when you trot out the lie. 'Honestly, he's fine,' you say, 'I love dogs.'

You don't love dogs and you certainly don't love being ravished by one in a suburban semi, but some combination of your Britishness and your upbringing leads you to tell the lie, and it's a lie you find yourself telling again and again. You tell it when you're up the park and a stranger's disgusting hound puts his head up your skirt; you tell it when you're by the canal and a filthy bundle of sinew paws you by the railings. You tell it at the seaside as a stinking yapper nudges you into the dunes, and you tell it in the pub garden as a bounding loon humps your leg to heaven by a patio heater. The dogs lunge and dribble and thrust and chew and all you can say is that everything is fine.

With the molester momentarily pacified you conclude the business for which you popped round (to borrow a drill, to share some coupons, to chuckle at a funny-shaped onion) then make your excuses to leave. Under the chair the dog appears to be sleeping, but as you rise from your seat he opens one eye and looks right through you to the very core of your frightened and quivering soul. You tiptoe down the hall, out the front door and into the cool air of the afternoon. And there, at the foot of the drive, stands a lusty bruiser with his crosshairs on your crotch. You smile at his flailing owner, close your eyes and prepare to tell him that it's really not a problem – you really, *really* love dogs.

LIE # **12**

" *I'll miss you.* **"**

Your partner is off! They're going on holiday to Barcelona with their best friend. You drive your partner to the airport. They are moved to tears by the separation. You don't feel the same but blink a lot to make your eyes go red.

'I'll miss you so much,' they say, sobbing.

'Ditto,' you reply.

'Will you really?' they ask.

'Of course,' you say, staring into their eyes. You're worryingly good at this.

Driving away from the airport your shoulders relax, a huge smile breaks out on that big round face of yours and your brain kicks into gear, running through all the exciting things you can do now that you have the freedom you've been craving for so long. These include:

Watch Heartbeat.
Drink wine for breakfast.
Flirt with your neighbour.
Move the sofa closer to the telly.

Not wipe the shower screen after use.
Order back-to-back takeaways.
Smoke cigarettes in the lounge.
Not make the bed.
Play your Genesis albums at full volume.
Eat on your lap and not at the table.
Go shopping and buy an outlandish shirt.
Have eight friends over at once.
Not have to go for a walk in the meadow on a Sunday.
Download Tinder on your phone.
Read your partner's diary.
Stay up until 4.17 a.m.

On the second day a great sadness washes over you. The source of the sadness, you realise while ordering your second Domino's pizza of the day, is that you are not missing your partner one iota. A genuine tear pricks your eye, before you wonder how you can get them to stay away longer. Perhaps you could say there's been a flood, or tell them that England is at war and they need to stay put until further notice.

On the third day you have truly hit your stride. The carpet is covered in underwear and discarded clothing, the plants are dying and not a single vegetable has passed your lips in forty-eight hours. In the space of two days you have turned single. You wonder whether this might in fact be the life for you, the single life. You could do what you like when you like, ideally in your underwear.

Perhaps you could even quit your job, get a flatmate and live off the rent.

'Surprise!' says your partner as they burst through the door wearing a sombrero.

'I thought you weren't back until this *evening*!' you exclaim, hurling a lit cigar out of an open window.

'Clearly,' they reply. 'This place is a tip! What have you been doing?'

'Missing you,' you say, downbeat.

'All of these empty bottles, all these takeaway boxes. Are you depressed?'

'I told you I missed you,' you reply, blinking a lot.

'Oh, my poor baby,' they say and hug you so hard you nearly bring up last night's doner meat and chips, extra chilli sauce please.

'You go and get a shower,' they say dumping their holiday bags. 'I'll tidy the place up a bit then we can go for a walk in the meadow.'

LIE # 13

" *I could have been a pro footballer, if it wasn't for my dodgy knee.* **"**

Every other bloke you meet claims to have had a trial for a professional football club, which is odd, considering that every other bloke you meet is terrible at football. If the chances of you ever seeing them play are slim they'll claim it was with Chelsea or Manchester United. They'll even throw in bits of colour to make their story sound true. Like the fact that Beckham used to do an extra hour's practice every day kicking pears at blackbirds he'd glued to the crossbar, or that Drogba loved playing Crash Bandicoot before a match. If there's any chance that you might actually see them play one day, say, at an office five-a-side, they'll choose a smaller club – Watford or Leyton Orient – and make a point of telling you how they knackered their knee which ended all hope of a pro-fessional career.

This made-up injury always happened dramatically. During a youth team FA Cup final they took out Shearer and got their leg stuck in an advertising board, or their kneecap exploded as they danced around Ashley Cole, or Bobby Charlton ran them over because they were too good at football. Whatever they say, it's always a lie. A genuine 'nearly man' says nothing when talk turns to football, the memory of the cruelly snatched dream being too painful to mention. But every now and then you might see them kick a roll of tape across a warehouse floor or chip a ball of screwed-up paper fifteen feet into a wastepaper basket. As the old saying goes: form is temporary, class permanent.

Other stupid bragging lies men like to tell other men include:

I used to be in the SAS.
At school I dumped Kelly Brook.
I have been banned from all the casinos in London because I know how to win.
I used to be in a band and we supported REM.
I once had a snog with an air hostess on a plane in that bit where they keep the foil dinners.
I had a fight with the games teacher at school and knocked him out.
I was approached by MI5 to be a secret agent.
I used to be a model, but then my face changed.
I stopped a bank robbery by wrestling a bloke with a shotgun to the floor and sitting on him until the police came.
I used to drive a Porsche but I gave it to my ex and just kept the Fiesta.

LIE # 14

" I'm not sure I'm well enough to go to school. "

Nobody can remember when their infant mind first makes the great leap into lying, but it must be around the point when you don't go to school for the first time because you are genuinely ill.

It's not on the first day of your illness; all your brain can think about then is how awful you feel, and how odd it is to be missing school. And it's not on the second day of your illness when you still feel quite poorly and don't go to school. No, the light-bulb moment happens on the third day, when actually you feel OK, but you still don't go to school. On that day you suddenly realise that nobody knows if you are really ill or not. There's no way of telling. The simple act of saying that you are ill means that everybody believes that you are ill. And once it dawns on you that just by saying you are ill you can get out of going to school, that's it. A lifetime of lying awaits you.

Of course, you soon learn that you have to be careful. There's a limit to how long you can get away with this tactic. Be 'ill' for more than three days in a row, and you

47

might end up at the doctor's, who will surely soon work out you are not ill. Do it too often and people will start to think you have some major disease and you'll end up in hospital having tests.

So it's something you have to save for special occasions, very specific things: when there's an exam you want to avoid; a particular teacher you can't stand; homework you haven't done; PE; Mondays.

You begin to develop little tricks to make your illness seem more real. Some are your own invention, some passed through the playground grapevine. A hot flannel on the forehead will make you feel hot. A thermometer in a cup of tea can make it look like you have a temperature.

You also begin to work out how you can build on your feelings of unease at going to school and turn them into 'bona fide' illnesses. So suddenly that hollow, pit-in-the-stomach feeling you have on a day with double maths – that really *is* a tummy ache. And the dread you have of rugby practice? That *is* a fever. You really feel it. YOU ARE ILL.

Later, you realise that the best technique is to not actually claim to be ill, but to wait for your parents to suggest that you are. So you limp slowly to the breakfast table, hunched, arms drooping, but in your school uniform. You just sort of stare at some toast for five minutes with a zombie-like gaze. You say nothing.

You wait until someone says: 'Are you feeling all right?'

Still you say nothing.

Then you get it again: 'I said, are you feeling all right?'

This time you sort of slur a reply. And then someone says it: 'I think you're coming down with something. I'm not sure you should go to school today.'

This is a brilliant technique, because you never actually lied in the first place. All you did was stare blankly at a box of cornflakes. You never said you were ill, *they* did.

A really advanced technique, as detailed in the brilliant *Whizzkid's Handbook* by Peter Eldin, takes this method to really advanced psychological depths. You sit at breakfast, with your head in your hands *when no one is watching you.* As soon as you spot an adult looking at you, you remove your hands and carry on as normal. When they look away you put your hands back. You have to wait until they say, 'Are you OK?' and you say, 'I'm fine'. Then you wait for them to say: 'I think you might have a headache – I'm not sure you can go to school.'

And so you don't, and you have a wonderful day at home reading books and watching daytime TV under a duvet.

And has it done you any harm? No. Except that you learned how to lie to get your own way.

And you failed your exams. And the best job you can get is in the Dixons at Gatwick South airside.

But it was all worth it, if only for the daytime TV under the duvet.

When is it OK to lie?

Rob:

I think in court, you know, when it matters.

David:

Yes, when it really gets you out of a tight spot.

Rob:

I'm a firm believer in the validity of the white lie in alleviating upset in a person, I think it's part of the lubrication of life. So in that sense, I do it.

David:

I think when someone has been rubbish in a play or a show, and you've gone to see it, my technique is to go, 'That was brilliant, you were the best thing in it.'

Rob:

Those were the words you used when you came to see me, I remember.

David:

I've been in some terrible things – I didn't know it at the time – and the next day I had to go on and do it again, and it wouldn't have helped if somebody had said something that made me feel like it was a complete waste of time. In that instance I think a white lie is fine, there's nothing to be gained from hurtful honesty.

Lee:

But you've got to draw the line somewhere haven't you? Like, if your wife says 'Does my bum look big in this?' the answer is always no. But if the question is 'Can I go in just knickers and a bra?' then you can't say, 'Of course, darling', you've got to say, 'No, you'll look mentally unhinged'. So it depends what's being asked doesn't it?

LIE # **15**

"*Not tonight, I've got a headache.***"**

The man is feeling amorous. Truth be told, the man was born amorous, which is why he found the woman. They started out feeling amorous together, then made the mistake of getting married. These days the man mostly feels amorous on his own, sometimes up to five times a day.

One night he decides to rekindle their romance via the power of intimate liaison. To show how serious he is, he removes first his socks, then Kevin Keegan wristbands, before finally unhooking his dollar medallion. He dims the lights, takes the copy of *Woman's Realm* from his wife's fingers and lightly places his tongue in her ear.

'Not tonight,' she says, 'I've got a headache.'

Chastened, the man shuffles back over to his side of the bed, picks up his Freemans catalogue and has a flick.

But guess what? The woman doesn't have a headache. She's barely had a headache in her life. The truth of the matter is she doesn't want to do it with her husband! But why not? There could be a number of explanations for her unwillingness:

She's tired.
She's gone off him.
She never liked him in the first place.
In fact, she can't stand him.
He has rabies and she doesn't want to catch it.
She has rabies and doesn't want to give it to him.
She's having an affair with his brother.
She's too engrossed in her article about women who
  stop having relations with their husbands.

This is not to say that the headache is solely the woman's preserve. Oh no. It is simply that a headache – unless a migraine – is a poor excuse. A vigorous cuddle is a superb method to distract from a headache. Just ask anyone who's done it with a hangover (or a supermodel).

There are of course a number of alternatives to the 'headache'. 'I'm too tired' is another favourite, along with 'It's been a long day' and 'I've got potato salad down below'. All are means by which to throw the partner off the scent. All are a lot kinder than: 'I'd rather have my eyes sucked out by industrial hoovers.'

While we may laugh at ways of avoiding intimacy, it remains a vital ingredient in any loving relationship (except for relationships with pets). Those that procrastinate rather than procreate are building tension and creating frustration within the partnership. It is therefore advisable that for every five 'headaches' there should be at least one 'go on, then'.

53

LIE # 16

"I'm not being . . ."

Any statement that begins with 'I'm not being . . .' is almost certainly a lie. In fact, it's hard to think of any statement that begins like this that isn't. Let's try.

'I'm not being . . . Miss Marple in the school production of *Murder at the Vicarage*.'

This might be true, though why anybody would turn down such a plum role is hard to fathom. Let's try and think of another one.

'I'm not being . . . blamed for the kidnap and false imprisonment of Simon Mayo, it was nothing to do with me. After all, I am Mark Kermode, his good friend and colleague!'

OK, I suppose this could be true. It seems unlikely that Mark Kermode would abduct and imprison his good friend Simon Mayo, especially as their movie review show is so popular with listeners of 5 live. But stranger things have happened. Let's try one more.

'I'm not being . . . photographed eating that bun. It belongs to Maureen Lipman!'

All right, this is almost certainly true; nobody in their right mind would willingly be photographed eating a bun that's been put aside for Maureen Lipman. As lovely as she is, she would be rightfully angered were a bun with her name on it taken by somebody else, and that anger could only be expected to rise were she presented with photographic evidence of the bun thief eating the sweet pastry. So, yes, I would argue that in this instance, the statement about not wanting to be photographed eating Maureen Lipman's bun is probably true.

Either way, I hope that I have skilfully proved here that these instances of truth are few and far between, for almost always the sentence that begins, 'I'm not being…' is a lie. Let's look at a few.

'I'm not being racist, but. . .'

Yes, you are. You are definitely about to be racist, but you hope that by saying you're not, your racist views will somehow appear more like common sense or universal truths. Well, you don't fool me, mister. You are a racist. Let's look at another one.

'I'm not being sexist, but . . .'

Yes, you are. You are definitely about to say something sexist, but you hope that by saying you're not people will mistake your misogyny for clear thinking. Well, you don't fool me, mister. You are a sexist. Let's try one more.

'I'm not being homophobic, but . . .'

55

Yes, you are. You are definitely about to make a homopho-bic comment, but you hope that by saying you're not nobody will notice that you're scared of other people's sexuality. Well, you don't fool me, mister. You are a homophobe.

A gentler way to try and get away with this lie is to say, 'I don't *mean* to be racist or homophobic, but . . .', the implication being that you are deeply troubled by the discovery of an absolute truth that just so happens to sound racist or homophobic, but one that needs telling nonetheless. If it were at all avoidable you wouldn't say it, but sometimes you just have to tell it like it is. You have to call a spade a spade. Or a gay spade if necessary. Well, you don't fool me. You, mister, are precisely what you're claiming not to be.

LIE # 17

" Sorry, I don't have any change on me. "

I mean I totally agree with what you're collecting for – earthquakes, sick donkeys, people who have less than we do (or any combination of those things). I really do. If only I had some change on me.

I can see you shaking your bucket in front of me. And I can see all the effort that you've gone to. With your costume and your loudhailer and your posters and your sad-looking face. It's just a real shame that I don't have any change on me.

And I really would like to give you some money towards it. It's a very worthy cause. If only I had some change on me.

But you don't know that I don't have any change on me. And I don't want you to think I'm a bad person. So I'm going to let you know: 'I've got no change on me.'

Now I bet you hear this sort of thing a lot, as you jangle your collection tin in front of hassled commuters. I bet a lot of people say they don't have any change when, actually, *they do*.

Well, I'm not one of those people. And to prove it, I'm

57

going to stick my hand in my pocket and sort of make a pronounced rummaging to the effect that my brain has suddenly thought: maybe I *do* have some change on me, if I have a really deep feel in that pocket. Yes, see, nothing. Let me really shake that pocket around so you can hear that there's absolutely nothing on me. Poor me. Poor you. Poor earthquakes/donkeys/poor people, etc.

Let me really jangle in there. Really poke the lining around in a way that is totally unnatural and looks slightly like I'm having a crafty fiddle.

(If I was a woman, this is the moment when I would pull out my purse and make a sort of Brechtian mime of finding nothing in it, despite staring really hard at it.)

Actually, I could have stuck my hand in my other pocket, where I'm pretty sure I would have found a pound coin. But that's not exactly change is it – a pound? That's sort of proper money. And I had marked it to buy some bread on the way home.

And I could have put my hand in my wallet and pulled out a note. But that's not change at all is it? That's actual money. That's *my* actual money. That's not change. That's not what you're interested in is it? That's not change. You want change.

And I just wish I had some on me.

LIE # 18

"I'm working from home tomorrow."

This is so common that it's not even considered a lie, it's taken for granted that all anyone who says it is going to do is keep an eye on their emails while awaiting the arrival of a dishwasher repairman.

Especially since, nowadays, with an iPhone, they don't even need to be at home to be not working from home. They can be not working from home in the pub, in the cinema or watching the 3.45 from Kempton Park in Ladbrokes. 'I'm working at home tomorrow' actually means 'I'm not working not at home tomorrow'.

But not *you*. *You're* not like these other dossers. *You* ARE 'working from home tomorrow'.

You say to anyone who will listen: 'I'm working from home tomorrow – I think I'll get more done.' (And it's just coincidence that the dishwasher repairman is coming.)

You rise excited and fire off your first email of the day. *Bleep*, off it goes. This is great. You are in charge of your own destiny. You are your own boss. You are master and servant.

That was a good song. 'Master and Servant' – Depeche Mode, wasn't it? You play a bit of it from YouTube. But you're not wasting time because, actually, without the commute, you're doing all this *before you would even have got to the office.* AMAZING!

You start work on your important document.

You write furiously, feverishly, brilliantly.

For nine minutes.

You pause.

You suddenly notice how completely and utterly alone you are.

Not just in the house.

In the universe.

It's like no one knows you exist.

You turn on the telly just to give yourself a bit of company.

It's *This Morning*, her from that programme is talking about that thing that was in the papers yesterday. Interesting . . .

Forty-five minutes later, you go back to the computer. You really are working from home, not like those other jokers.

The post drops through the door.

Oh, so this is what time the postman comes.

Does he want to have a chat, perhaps? He knows you exist. Otherwise why would he have put that gas bill through the postbox?

You open the door but he's gone.

You go back to your computer.

What time is it? Is it almost lunchtime? It's 11.18 a.m. – is that almost lunchtime?

Then the dishwasher man arrives and you have a chat with him and he needs to come back with a part and now it really is lunchtime so you eat in front of the first of a repeat of a whole week's worth of *Come Dine With Me* on Channel 4+1 and you end up watching the next one as well and the one after that because it really is quite funny actually and anyway the dishwasher man is going to be back at any point and ah, there he is, you might as well watch the last *Come Dine With Me*.

You go back to the computer.

You realise that you have left something you need in the office. You'll get someone to bike it to you, but it won't get to you for a bit so probably the best thing now is to go and watch the 3.45 from Kempton Park in Ladbrokes, then nip to the supermarket and be back in time for *Pointless*.

But you do have a lot of stuff to sort out. There's only one thing for it. You'll have to send one last email to the office:

'I'm working from home tomorrow.'

As comedy writers you are legitimately allowed to work from home. Do you find you get easily distracted?

David:

I have a book called *Willesden Past*, which is a local history of the Kilburn/Willesden area. I find it very distracting in a work environment, and yet in pure leisure time I'm not drawn to it.

Rob:

I have a similar book that focuses on Richmond, but almost entirely ignores Willesden.

Lee:

I have a book genuinely called *Potty, Fartwell and Knob*, which is about all the unusual surnames in the country.

Rob:

Well that says everything: David reads local history, I read local history, Lee reads *Potty, Fartwell and Knob*.

Lee:

Don't knock it. There's a good section on the Tits of Hampstead.

LIE # 19

"Of course I've read *Ulysses*."

You may have heard that ignorance is bliss, but in fact it is an acutely embarrassing state of factual absence. Admitting that you don't know what a cumquat is (it's a rare mammal), why a tomato is a fruit (because it's red) or what the capital of Chile is (Mexico City – I didn't even have to look that one up) may lead to social exclusion and, in exceptional circumstances, indigestion.

In order to disguise our ignorance we will often claim to have seen/read/heard/done/eaten/slept with things we haven't. This may mean lying about the films of Kurosawa, faking an appreciation of the works of Brahms or, for literary folk, pretending to have read *Ulysses* by William Hemingway (I think that's right).

You're at a dinner party. The hosts are serious readers. You like to read, though you also enjoy making mud pies, pulling silly faces and rolling up and down hills. Upon arriving at their grand house you see clearly just how important books are to them, partly because of the hundreds of examples on their shelves but also because there's a big poster on the wall that says: TO US BOOKS ARE IMPORTANT.

You are fond of your hosts. You should like to remain friends with them both, perhaps even develop the friendship further because you enjoy their company and find them both arousing. To do so you feel it is important to agree with what they say, feign similar interests and not draw attention to the dark recesses of ignorance that reside in your hollow brain and haunt your waking hours.

'We simply ad*ore* Vienna!' they say.

'So do we!' you reply.

'Isn't Modigliani just wonderful?'

'Isn't it!' you say.

'Don't you feel *Ulysses* is both the beginning and the *end* of all literature?'

'You rotter!' you chime. 'I was just about to say that!'

What a dolt you are, talking about a book you've never read in that fashion. You've left yourself open. This is what happens when you agree with people willy-nilly. The woman smiles back at you, then gives you a curious look.

'Tell us, just why is it you enjoy *Ulysses* quite so much?' she enquires.

Now you're stuck.

'Are you asking me why it is that I enjoy *Ulysses* quite so much?' you say, playing for time.

'Yes,' she replies.

You now have three options: come clean, ask where the bathroom is or make something up. Inevitably, you choose the last of these.

'It's the sheer, and forgive me . . . *Ulyssesian* way the poem plays itself out,' you say.

There is a pause, during which the couple look at each other, remove their glasses in tandem and rub their eyes.

'It's a *novel*,' the woman replies curtly, 'not a *poem*.'

'To *you* maybe,' you counter. 'To me it is a paean to the heart, and for this reason I have always read it as a poem.'

You cannot hide the sheer joy at your use of the word 'paean', which you looked up before you left the house.

'*Interesting* . . .' she says. 'Do you feel it bears comparison . . . to his *later* work?'

You think about this. You stop talking and you think. You saw Tony Parsons do this once on *Late Review* so you know it shows gravitas. Slowly, you collect your thoughts, dab at the edges of your mouth with the linen napkin and speak.

'It's certainly a *lot* better than *Bravo Two Zero*,' you reply. 'Loads better, in fact.'

And you were getting on so well.

LIE # 20

"It's research."

Almost everyone has at some stage or another said: 'I'm thinking of writing a book, a play, a film or something.'

They may have done nothing more than that, just 'thought' that they might write something in the future.

And from the moment they say they are 'thinking' of doing that, they can allow themselves to do anything that might otherwise appear unnecessary, ill-advised, stupid or just plain wrong with two words: 'It's research.'

So they can say to themselves:

'Hey, I'm going to see that brain-dead, clichéd, predictable action movie. I know it's trash but *it's research* for a brain-dead, clichéd, predictable action movie script I'm thinking I might write.'

Or, 'Hey, I'm going to watch all of *EastEnders* forever for the rest of my life. I know it's rubbish but *it's research* for a rubbish soap opera I'm thinking of writing.'

Or, 'Hey, I'm going to read this simple-minded, large-print, semi-erotic rom-com novel that has a picture on the cover that's exactly the same as all the other simple-minded, large-print, semi-erotic rom-com novels because *it's research* for the simple-minded, large-print, semi-erotic rom-com novel I'm thinking of writing that will have exactly the same cover as all the other simple-minded, large-print, semi-erotic rom-com novels.'

You don't have to be actually doing any of these things, you don't even need to have an idea for a thing, you just need to be 'thinking of' doing a thing.

'It's research' is a self-delusional lie that, in expert hands, can allow for all sorts of behaviour that would otherwise be considered questionable.

'Hey, I'm going to play FIFA 14 all day and night for a month, because *it's research* for a contemporary novel I'm thinking of writing about someone who plays FIFA 14 all day and night for a month.'

Or, 'Hey, I'm going to get a job in arms sales. *It's research* for a rap I'm think of writing about landmines.'

Or even, 'Hey, I'm going to tell a lot of lies. *It's research* for a book about lies I'm thinking of writing.'

And you're reading it right now. Possibly because it's research.

Make sure you keep the receipt for your accountant.

LIE # 21

"I have no idea why my laptop isn't working."

So your laptop isn't working. Nothing happens when you try to turn it on. So you call the service centre.

They're very helpful. Yes, you have tried turning it on and off again.

But have you tried turning it on again while holding down the Command+Alt+Shift keys, they suggest? Still nothing happens.

They say it looks like you have a hardware fault. Something that needs a repair. Don't worry, it's all covered by your guarantee. They'll send a courier to collect it, then fix it and send it back to you. It won't cost you a penny. They can send someone to pick it up tomorrow. That *is* good service, you think. If a laptop has to go wrong, then at least it's being repaired as quickly and painlessly as possible.

They'll set up the whole thing. But there's just one thing they need to ask first: 'Do you know if it could have been damaged?'

Before they've even got to the end of the sentence something crosses your mind. Didn't you sort of accidentally drop it the other day? It sort of flew out of your hands as you put it in your bag? Could that have been the cause? No, it seemed to be working after that. It can't be that. Best not mention it.

'You haven't dropped your laptop at all?'

'. . . No.'

Then a few days after that there was the incident where you packed your swimming kit in with your laptop and the top of your Cherry Tango shower gel came off and everything was covered in pink gunk. You made sure you wiped it all off, especially round the USB port. It can't be that. Surely. If anything it actually made the computer a bit cleaner.

'You haven't spilt any liquids on the laptop?'

'. . . No.'

Should you mention the shower gel incident? Probably not. It's probably nothing to do with it. Although it probably *is* something to do with it. As long as they don't swab it for Cherry Tango then there won't be a problem. And why would they swab it for Cherry Tango?

But he knows. You think he already knows. The sound of your voice has flagged their lie-detecting software and your call has been logged by a CIA cyber-terrorism alert in a square building near a car park in West Virginia. They're on to you. They're only keeping you talking so they can get a fix on your GPS co-ordinates.

'And, so, sir, you have no knowledge of why your computer has broken? I just have to ask. You have no idea how many people suddenly realise that they dropped it or something.'

Do you crack? No knowledge? Well, you don't have any actual knowledge of what's wrong with it, so how could you have any knowledge of why it isn't working? You don't want to lie to them, but well, it could have been the fact you dropped it on the floor then spilt a bottle of bright pink liquid soap on it, but you don't *know* that for sure. And anyway, even if it that was the cause, they make loads of money, they can afford to fix one laptop. But what if they open it up and it's full of Cherry Tango shower gel? Then they'll know. But maybe it won't be full of Cherry Tango shower gel. So in the split second you have to answer you say:

'. . . No. I have no idea why my laptop isn't working.'

And the man on the other end of the line makes a note against your claim: 'Suspicious'.

LIE # 22

"That smell – it wasn't me!"

Passing wind, barking, 'blowing off'. Call it what you like, we all do it. Along with lying, crying and learning to drive it's part of what makes us human. Other mammals do it too, though they are less concerned about the outcome and tend to 'toot their horn' willy-nilly.

Man, on the other hand, chooses when to 'blast off'. Ideally this takes place within a bathroom environment, at a blustery school fete or in bed when his partner is asleep and he can have a long, satisfying inhalation. Note: the choice of *when* to break wind diminishes sharply beyond the age of seventy.

The challenge arises when the hazardous honker (you) is full to the meniscus with gas and in a group scenario. Here, the overriding question is: do I know these people? If you do not (in a lift/at a barn dance/speed dating) chances are you can chuff as long and hard as you wish and no one will say a word. They may pull a face and raise their fingers to their nose as if to say, 'My word, that's a ripper, and by the way, it wasn't me – but, unless you're a vegan, the trump is unlikely to garner verbal protest. Denial is unnecessary.

71

A public arena where you are known is more complex. Let's say the area around your work desk reeks of methane. No one would dare light a match there. This amuses your colleagues, but one day the MD comes over. She approaches with a view to congratulating you on last month's sales figures and to offer you a promotion, only to depart a minute later feeling nauseous and wondering whether you are indeed the person to fill the role in the Middle East.

'Wasn't me!' you cry out.

The MD turns.

'That trouser trumpet!' you say. 'It wasn't me! It was Judith from HR! She was here just before you arrived. She had Indian last night!'

The MD walks back to your desk.

'He who smelt it dealt it,' she says before turning on her heels, handkerchief covering her face.

A further situation where cutting the cheese may prove problematic is in the presence of a partner. After eight months it is common for the man to relax his attitude in front of the lady. Unfortunately, double standards dictate that she may not reciprocate. Early in a relationship it is anathema for either to drop an air biscuit in the presence of the other. Should this occur, denial is vital.

'Did you just beep your horn?'
'The drains round here are terrible. Apparently they're Victorian.'
'I heard it.'

'That's my pet duck.'
'You've got a pet duck?'
'Yes.'
'Where is he?'
'It's a she – and she flew off.'
'Ducks can't fly.'
'Yes, they can.'
'No, they can't.'
'Enough of this nonsense, would you like me to buy you
    dinner, drinks and a new dress?'

The truth is that on occasion we all feel angry at the world
– its injustice, hardships; its very toughness. Sometimes
a silent protest may put us back on track. Just be careful:
gauge your audience, choose your moment and never,
ever strain.

LIE # 23

" My salary at my previous job " was . . .

The interview is going well. You started with a strong handshake and remembered to let go. You said you could bring a lot to the role and read three examples from your palm. You even told your knock, knock jokes, one of which got big laughs.

'What is your current salary?' they enquire.

No one's ever asked you this before. It must be because they want to offer you the job!

'£650,000,' you reply without hesitation.

'That's certainly above the market rate,' they say, 'for a glove salesman.'

'My glove salesmanship is first rate,' you reply. 'It's very probable that I'm the best glove salesman in Solihull.'

'Is that so?'

'Very much,' you say. 'And I am rewarded in line with my results and ability.'

'Mmm,' they say.

'Thanks,' you reply.

You wouldn't be the first person to inflate your net worth. The temptation to add a few thousand to your current earnings when the opportunity arises invariably proves too great. Most succumb. Some are executed at dawn, while others slip through the net unnoticed.

'Honesty is very important in our business,' they continue. 'If we feel you are being dishonest in any way that would make matters, shall we say, *complicated*.'

'Obvs,' you reply.

'Presumably, if we asked your existing company your current salary they would quote the same figure.'

You hold their stare and sigh.

'Not exactly, but that's because for the most part they pay me cash in hand.'

'For the most part?'

'Ninety-eight per cent.'

'That is indeed the most part.'

'Exactly.'

They fix you with a steely glare.

'You do realise this is *illegal*?'

'Don't I know it,' you reply, rolling your eyes. 'Problem is, there's no telling them. I say, "Please don't pay cash, I'd rather earn the dollar and declare it. Also what happens if I go for a job interview and need to prove how much I earn? It won't look good will it?"'

'No, it won't,' they say.

'Thanks,' you reply.

What if you're being underpaid in your current role? If you quote your real salary they'll use that as a starting point. But you don't want to start there; you want to start higher up the chain because you're a winner! You deserve more. All you're doing is bridging the gap for them. They should be grateful; it will only serve to motivate you onto even greater heights.

'Let's say, for the sake of argument, you *do* earn £650,000 a year.'

'Which I do,' you reply.

'The role we're interviewing for goes up to £33,500 per annum, plus benefits.'

'What are the benefits?'

'Free torch.'

'Oh yeah.'

'There is considerable shortfall between what we can offer and what you claim to be currently earning.'

'What do you mean, "shortfall"?'

'Discrepancy.'

'Keep going.'

'*Difference.*'

'Oh yeah.'

'There's not much in it for you, Mr Splonge, if you leave your current position. With us you will earn £616,500 *less* than you do in your current position.'

You pause for a moment.

'How big is the torch?'

'Medium-sized,' they reply.

'Batteries included?'

'Could be arranged.'

'When do I start?'

76

24

"No, I don't smoke."

Nobody likes going to the doctor's. Apart from hypochondriacs and people who are having affairs with doctors. For everybody else, it's a pain in the neck. Which is sometimes the reason they are there.

First of all you have to register at the desk with a receptionist who hates you for being in her proximity while potentially contagious. Then, as you lean on the counter trying not to cough in her face, you notice you're leaning next to the stool sample box. For a brief moment your mind idly wonders whose poos are inside it and what hideous fogs they are emitting. Suddenly, you are woken from this daydream by a pensioner sneezing on your hand.

You take your seat in the waiting room and look around at the people already sat there. There's a fat man in a tracksuit blowing his nose, and a toddler asking his mother to explain the cover of a two-year-old copy of *Private Eye*. In one corner a television with the sound turned down is showing an episode of *The Jeremy Kyle Show*. Somebody on it is cross with somebody else but thankfully Jeremy is there to take the heat out of the situation. You wonder if the waiting room for hell is a bit like this. But why should you care? You're not going to hell. You've given money to Comic Relief and once helped your elderly neighbour carry a table up some stairs.

You look around at the posters on the walls and contemplate the diseases they are advertising. They sound pretty grim. Maybe your sore throat is more than just a cold. Maybe you've got AIDS. You play a game of Angry Birds and think about that waiting room for hell.

A bing-bong sound goes bing-bong and everybody looks up to see whose bing has been bonged. According to the display it's you. Others in the waiting room audibly tut as you make your way to the consulting room.

You enter the room coughing. It's not entirely put on, but you up the volume a touch and frown a bit more than usual to show the doctor you really are in pain and not wasting her time. She seems unimpressed, almost bored in fact. You force a smile, take a seat and begin to tell her about your ailments.

As you run through your catalogue of complaints – sore throat, achy limbs, a headache and, worst of all, a rattle in your chest – you can't help noticing how young she seems. How did she get to be a doctor and pass all those exams that doctors have to pass and still be considerably younger than you? Maybe she's not the actual doctor, maybe this is a hidden camera show for ITV2 and any minute now Keith Lemon is going to climb out of a cupboard and present you with a prize. You start looking around the room for hidden cameras or signs of Keith, but before you know it she's looking down your throat with a tiny torch and pressing a cold stethoscope onto your back.

She tells you you've got a cold and that there's not much you can do apart from take some paracetamol, drink plenty of water and get some rest. But, she says, as you are a person of a certain age she just wants to ask you a few questions. First up, do you smoke?

Now, this is a tricky one to answer. You did smoke, *did*, but that was a while ago and you don't any more. Well, at least you don't buy them any more. You sometimes have one at a party, after you've had a few, if there's something to celebrate, but that's not very often and you usually end up dancing, which is like exercising and so balances out the bad bits of the fags. Occasionally, very occasionally, you have one after work, or at lunchtimes, stood in the rain in a doorway with Karen, but that's mainly because Karen likes smoking and doesn't want to stand in that doorway on her own, so they don't really count. They're sociable smokes, not needy ones. You don't *need* to smoke ever, you just choose to sometimes. Like yesterday morning, when the train was late, and last night after you got all cross when your favourite one was booted off *Masterchef*. Or this morning when you couldn't sleep because of your cold and you found an old packet of ten at the back of a cupboard while rummaging about for a Lemsip. You couldn't think of anything worse, but once you'd found them you remembered that chat you had with Stu at university. He said his dad knew some professor or something who said that the best way to clear a chest infection was to smoke it out with a few ciggies. Stu swore by it as a cure. It sounded daft at the time, but nothing else was working and you were up at 5 a.m. with nothing else to do. So you stood by the kitchen door smoking a few fags and watching the sun come up over the graveyard. But that's not proper smoking. That was medicinal.

Anyway, it's a stupid question. Nobody would tell a doctor that they smoke. Not even if they were a proper smoker, rather than the sociable, self-medicating type, like you. Why on earth do they even ask the question? Maybe they want to tell the government. Or even worse, your parents.

'No,' you say. 'I don't smoke.'

'Have you ever?' she asks, like someone cleverer than you.

'No,' you say, and the lie lands with a thud on the table and both of you pretend you haven't seen it.

Have you ever lied to your doctor?

Lee:

I often lie when they ask you to fill out a form, because I'm 5 foot 11 and three-quarters, but I can't bring myself not to be 6 foot, so I always put 6 foot. But also, I reckon sometimes I might be 6 foot. You know, because you shrink in the day, don't you. You're smaller at the end of the day than you are at the beginning.

David:

Yes, you're taller lying down.

Lee:

In the old days you were meant to be a certain height to be a policeman. If people were too short, they'd say come back tomorrow morning and be measured again, and suddenly they were tall enough. Because you shrink during the day, some people could get in the police force in the morning but not in the evening.

David:

Nowadays there's no height restriction at all, hence all the dwarf policeman letting criminals run rife.

Lee:

Ah, but they've changed the rules though, haven't they? Now they measure how high you have to be to be a burglar.

Rob:

All this talk of height is very upsetting, can we move on.

LIE # 25

" I'm going to start jogging . . . tomorrow. "

Some people jog today, and some people jog tomorrow. But if you go to the park tomorrow you'll only see the people who are jogging today. That's not because you've slipped through a space–time wormhole, but because the people who say they will start jogging tomorrow are liars. They don't think of themselves as liars, they think of themselves as future joggers, but we know they're liars because today they are eating pizza and today used to be tomorrow. But that was yesterday.

You can always tell a future jogger because they tend to have all the kit. Real joggers can do it in anything – a pair of old shorts and a knackered T-shirt – but the future jogger needs to spend a lot of time ordering stuff online so that they really look the part when they get down the park tomorrow. High-vis clothing, water bottles, jogger's sunglasses, heart-monitoring wristbands, nipple-chaffing cream and a copy of *The Procrastinator's Guide to Jogging: A Step-by-Step Guide* are all necessary purchases before mud can be allowed to meet training shoe.

Then there's the jogger's playlist that needs compiling. You can't just run with the wind in your ears, you need motivational music to get you past the duck pond. A bit of Coldplay here, a bit of some other dick there – the future jogger can spend a good few weeks compiling a playlist to accompany the aspirational montage sequence playing inside their head.

But let's not be too hard on the jogger dodgers. Have you been to the park of late and watched the procession of puffers pounding the paths? Nothing about it or them looks fun. The odd one or two look like they know what they're doing, but the vast majority appear to be taking part in a Nincompoop in Shorts competition. And they're all winning. Here comes one now, trotting through the trees like a constipated frog; there goes another, wheezing his way to the water fountain dreaming of biscuits. The sun comes up and the sun goes down, and round and round the fringes of the green they lope, each in search of a time when their bodies worked. Back in their kitchens they raid the fridge for carrot batons and peck at packets of seeds like mad parrots. A glass of green bog water and a Swedish cracker later and they're ready for the shower. A chance to wash away the memory of what just happened and to try and forget that tomorrow it will happen again. Is it any surprise that some of us prefer to stay in bed watching videos of cats on skateboards?

If you're bored of telling yourself the jogging lie remember there are plenty of other ways to avoid getting the blood pumping. You can pretend you're about to go swimming as soon as you've found the right pool, that you're about to start jiving as soon as you've found the right partner, or that you're about to start Zumba as soon as you've found a place to leave your dignity. But best of all, you could take a long hard look in the mirror and tell yourself you love you just the way you are, draw the curtains and climb back into bed.

LIE# 26

"I'm well, thanks.**"**

Isabelle and Luke are moving to Ipswich so they've thrown a party. You wished they hadn't because you hate parties, as well as hating Isabelle and Luke. But you're here now so might as well make the best of it. Who knows, perhaps you'll get drunk again and go through their underwear drawer.

You arrive, are ushered through to the kitchen, pour yourself a drink, down it in one, grab another and thread your way out into the garden. There you spot a person you don't entirely despise and make a beeline for them.

'And how are *you*?' they ask.

'I'm well, thanks!'

You keep smiling but the smile doesn't reach your eyes. You wish you were well. You'd like to be well. In fact, you would be well if only:

You weren't in the middle of an acrimonious divorce.
You hadn't started experiencing panic attacks when
   driving over high bridges.
You could feel your right leg.

You had a job.
You didn't lug around with you a mysterious sadness
    dating back to your childhood.
You didn't hate everyone there, especially the smug lady
    with the two irritating kids and the 'incredible' job.
You weren't consumed by hate.
You lost three stone.
You hadn't been given only twenty-six years to live.
You had a sense of purpose.
You didn't snort then cough when you laughed.

'Excellent!' they reply, looking past your ear.

'And you?' you ask, because you've done this enough times to know how it works.

'Me? I'm good, thanks!'

They look OK, though you think you might be able to detect a hint of desperation in the corners of their eyes.

'So you're good?' you reiterate.

'Yes!' they reply. But they are unable to hold your eyes for more than a second. It must be because they are:

In £961,000 of debt.
Fathering a child with a woman they've only ever met
    in a toilet.
Suffering an existential crisis.
Worried people can see how old their shoes are.
Still guilty about hitting that horse with a plastic
    lightsabre in 1982.

On a warning at work for logging into other people's
   emails and sending explicit donkey images to clients.
Addicted to syrup.
Afraid of ceilings.
Convinced everyone at the party knows about the
   incident with the policeman.
Convinced their least favourite uncle is actually their
   father.
Hung-over.
Sad about their hair.
Consumed by their fallen arches.

'Great!' you say. 'Look at us! Both so well!'

'Aren't we!' they reply. 'Hey listen, hope you don't think me *too* rude but I *so* need to go and speak to Susan over there? With the adorable kids? Apparently she's got this am-*azing* house in France and I want to hear *all* about it. Catch you later?'

You are deserted and stand motionless. A woman you haven't seen in years approaches .

'How are you?' she asks.

'I'm well, thanks!' you lie. 'And you?'

'Not good,' she replies. 'Not good at all.'

'Sorry, but I need the bathroom,' you say, and exit.

LIE # 27

" The cheque's in the post. "

'The cheque's in the post' regularly tops surveys of common lies. But how can it? No one sends cheques any more.

If someone said to you, 'The cheque's in the post', you'd know they were lying because *no one knows where their chequebook is any more.* How can someone really have put a cheque in the post to you when they don't even know where their chequebook is?

(Also, no one has envelopes any more. No one knows where the postbox is. No one has anyone to send a cheque to, nobody has any stamps on them and even if they did, no one knows how many stamps to put on anything ever since the Royal Mail changed all the rules and made the postage all about how big the envelope is.)

And similarly, no one actually wants to receive a cheque these days. What are you meant to do with it? Take it to a bank!? Actually go to an actual bank – (where is it?) – and actually go and stand in an actual line in an actual bank and fill in a form and say hello to someone and actually hand it to them!? Are you actually mad?

Giving someone a cheque when you owe them money is the safest way of not giving someone the money.

In fact, cheerily saying the words 'Here is that cheque for the money I owe you' is a more common deceit than 'The cheque's in the post'. It's a lie because you actually suspect they will never pay it in. You're basically saying to the person who you owe the money to: 'Are you prepared to spend all day paying this cheque for £13.45 into your account? Or is it just going to sit on your bedside table for three months until you give up and tear it into little bits and throw it in the bin?'

(People always tear cheques up into little bits, taking care to tear through the sort code, before they throw it away. This is in case burglars break in and decide to go through the bin sellotaping cheques for trivial amounts together, rather than just nicking your laptop.)

Even though electronic payments mean that 'the cheque's in the post' is an anachronism, as a concept it still remains. Last year it was estimated that British businesses are, at any one time, owed £30 billion in late payments. That's a lot of cheques supposedly in the post. And that might explain why, as a lie, it remains in people's heads, because the alternatives seem less appealing. 'The Bankers' Automated Clearing Services transfer has been set up' or 'The Bankers' Automated Clearing Services transfer is pending' don't have quite the same ring to them.

Exercises

1. Where is your chequebook? Are you sure? Take a look. See, it's not where you thought it was. Try to find it without phoning your mum.

2. What is the correct postage for a letter that is 30 cm x 15 cm? Asking for a friend.

3. Where is the nearest branch of your bank? Try to pay in a cheque from a friend without feeling worthless and mean.

LIE # 28

"Your food doesn't have to be served on a plate."

In the good old days before Keith Lemon and ISIS, food was served on plates.

It just seemed to work. But when a gastropub chef, unable to find a clean plate because the washer-upper had died in a tent at Glastonbury, served a burger and fries on a chopping board, a new phase in culinary idiocy began.

Suddenly, dining out became a game of Russian roulette. Yes, I would quite like the sausage and mash, but will it be served in a top hat? The risotto sounds nice, but I'm not sure I want to spoon it off a Janis Joplin LP. Soup in an ashtray, you say? I think I'll try next door.

As an act of public service, this book is here to take a stand. People have had enough. They just want their dinners on plates. No more roof tiles, skillets, breadboards or trays. And to any restaurant manager thinking of getting really creative, the following suggestions are equally unacceptable.

Chips in gloves

Two leather driving gloves stuffed finger deep with hand-cut, skin-on chips.

Ladies' gloves £4   Men's gloves £7

A box file of broth

An old box file (previously used by the Ministry of Defence) full to the brim with two-day-old broth.

Serves 4   £20

Beef balaclava

A premium 8 oz Angus beef steak, secreted in a black woollen balaclava. Served with one giant chip.

£15

Bubble-wrapped haddock

Locally sourced haddock, unwashed and wrapped head-to-fin in grade-one bubble wrap. Comes with a bubble of ketchup and a bubble of salt (no pepper).

£13.50

Strawberries and cream on a tennis racket

Only available for the second week of Wimbledon, this pudding comes without cutlery – eat it straight from the racket! For an additional charge, the management are happy to provide a bib.

Pudding £7   Bib £3.50

Potty mash

A plastic potty (unused) heaped with mustard mash and gravy. Best eaten straight from the potty.

£4.50

A binocular case of wasabi peas

A vintage leather field-glasses case bloated with spicy wasabi balls.

£6.11

P45 Cajun chicken

Delicious strips of chicken casually tossed onto the P45 of an ex-employee.

£9

Ham in a shoe

Ham from Ipswich rehoused in a hand-stitched leather brogue.

Size 8: £6   Size 9: £10   Size 12: £11.01

Chicken Caesar hairnet

Delicious free-range chicken drizzled with the chef's special Caesar sauce and cradled in a ladies hairnet.

£12

Steak and ale pie in an old Cluedo box

A vintage meal in a vintage box (note, the spanner is missing and Colonel Mustard's nose has worn off).

£9.50

A Brabantia bin of pulled pork

A 30-litre brushed-steel Brabantia kitchen bin lined with rice paper then stuffed with organically reared pulled pork.

Serves 8   £65

Pizza on a manhole cover

A 12-inch margherita pizza served on a manhole cover that used to sit outside Harold Pinter's house.

£11

When filming _Would I Lie To You?_ how easy do you find it to turn over a card you've genuinely never seen before and tell a lie?

Lee:

I would say that it's much easier to tell a lie because we lie all the time. You say things like 'I like your shirt' and you don't really mean it or 'Lovely to see you!' when it's just all right to see someone. Our lives are full of lies from the minute we get up until the minute we go to bed. But there is never a situation in real life where you are required to tell the truth, but make it look like a lie, like you have to with a true statement on the show. That situation never crops up, ever.

David:

Yes, there's no practice for that.

Lee:

No, so you're not trained for that on the show. I can't think of any situation in the history of mankind where you tell the truth and try and sell it as lie. Nobody has ever thought, 'Oh, I've got to tell my wife the truth but I hope to God she thinks I'm lying.'

David:

No, but it's an interesting technique if you've been having an affair and you decide to come clean. You know, you've got to do it so implausibly that your wife says, 'No, you haven't.' [Impersonates a hesitant man] 'Ah, look dear, I've, um, secretly been having an affair with, er, *four*, I think it's *four* other women.' But you sound so fake she just says, 'No, no, no, this marriage has never been more solid', and you think to yourself, well I've come clean and she seems to have got over it so, fine, we can move on.

Lee:
That's a good idea.

David:
'Listen, darling, I have a whole other family with, er, three children, and that's where I am when I say I'm at work' … let's say. Oh, and: 'I have [*gives a little chuckle*] killed twice.'

LIE # 29

"You have won the Nigerian lottery!"

Most people are wise to this scam now. They quickly press delete when an email comes through suggesting that they have won the Nigerian lottery, or are the only person who can claim millions in a dormant bank account, providing that they send a complete stranger a few thousand dollars to cover expenses.

They know they're never going to see any money even if they pay up, and that they will be asked to pay up more and more money for 'expenses' until eventually they never hear from their mysterious Nigerian contacts again.

But the scam didn't begin with the invention of the internet. It's a type of ruse known as the advance-fee con and as long ago as the sixteenth century charlatans were trying their luck with what became known as the Spanish Prisoner scam.

In this version, a shadowy conman would offer a punter the chance to help release a mysterious, wealthy nobleman from a prison in Spain by paying off his guards – for which the punter would be richly rewarded by the thankful noble. Of course, more money is always required, the noble is never released and the punter is rinsed of his money until he is penniless.

But the arrival of email meant that instead of having to approach naive-looking punters in taverns, scammers could send off millions of initial approaches in seconds. Even though most people simply delete them, and only a tiny percentage of people follow up the scam letter, that's enough to keep the conmen in business.

Although this type of con is inexorably connected with Nigeria, it actually accounts for only a small proportion of internet fraud. The vast majority of internet fraud originates in the United States, with Nigeria accounting for only around 6 per cent.

It's hard to work out how successful these cons are – but the fact that they keep going suggests it's worth the conmen's while. The victims often never come forward once they realise they have been taken for a ride, such is their embarrassment.

And maybe they are right to maintain a low profile. One variation of the scam preys upon previous victims. Known as a reloading scam, shady figures get in touch with victims to say they can catch the scammer who initially conned them and get their money back. All they have to do is send a few thousand dollars through to cover expenses . . .

LIE # 30

“I'm five minutes away.**”**

You're running late. You're always running late. What a git you are. You've spent your life making other people wait and today is no exception. You text ahead: 'Five minutes.'

Except it's not five minutes is it, you scrote? It's ten. Ten? It may even be fifteen. Fifteen minutes! You're a rotter. One of the people waiting for you has the flu. Another was born with a curled-up foot. Everyone knows you're not even close. While your friends are hopping from foot to curled-up foot just to keep warm you amble aimlessly down Dunstable High Street, stopping to pat a cat or watch the telly in the TV-rental shop.

Like so many modern-day twits you believe that portable phone technology bestows upon the individual the license to show up tardy. You've lost sight of old-fashioned notions such as 'respect', 'consideration' and 'not being late for everything like a willy'. Instead you live in your own idiotic bubble, insisting people work around you, kowtow to your schedule, dance to your tune and jive to your groove. You're not even musical, for God's sake.

Eight minutes pass. You fire off another text – 'Nearly there!' – knowing full well it's ten minutes, even if you trot. What happened to you? You're thirty-eight! You can't keep doing this to people. They'll get sick of you. As it is you're quite boring so you really can't afford to test people's patience. I wasn't going to mention it, but I think you should know.

You pick up the pace and start jogging, while simultaneously liking a picture of a cockatoo on Facebook. Head down, you plough into a pensioner. They're on their back, apples everywhere, crying for their late husband. This is going to take a while. You dig out your phone: 'Stuck in traffic. ETA 3.15!'

You're a gutless twerp. You don't have the gumption to relay the full truth: that you are, and always were going to be, nineteen minutes late. No one likes a coward, least of all a boring one (did I mention that you're boring?). Man up. Stop weaselling. Get a life.

The frustrating thing is, it's really easy to be on time. You simply write the time you need to be somewhere on your hand or other hand, calculate how long it will take to get there, factor in the stuff you need to do beforehand, then set off. 'I know!' you cry, late for the dentist by a week. 'But it's the phone! It's *making* me late!'

In the days before mobiles the world ran like clockwork. If you had to be somewhere at an appointed time you made sure you were. More than fifteen minutes late and it was assumed you were dead. Entire funerals could be arranged for those who arrived forty minutes late. Today, people – especially *young* people (i.e. idiots) – alert others electronically as to their whereabouts, letting them down in increments of five minutes in the hope that they won't be entirely despised when they finally arrive. Frankly, it's not good enough.

We all know 'five minutes' never means five minutes, just as 'I like your collection of rare Yes EPs' never means 'I like your collection of rare Yes EPs'.

Isn't it time we changed this preposterous social convention? Why not surprise everyone by arriving on time for a change? Set off in advance, don't dilly-dally, walk at a steady pace, no need to text ahead.

Well done, you did it!

Oh.

There's no one else here.

Just you and three texts that say: 'Five minutes.'

Lies to watch out for from . . . **Pop Stars**

LIE # 31

"I think this is the best record I've ever made."

When a pop star from a much-loved band makes a solo record, they like to spew this particular lie all over the broadsheets; and the worse the record, the bigger the splat of the spew. Time to take most cover is when they are promoting a 'world music' record. You know the sort of thing, they've hooked up with a Nigerian percussionist and an Icelandic harpist to record a collection of haikus daubed on the walls of a Tibetan prison cell. On first listen you think there might be a fault with the CD; on second listen you still think there's a fault with the CD. It takes a live performance on *Late Review* and some high praise from Paul Morley to convince you that that's what it's meant to sound like, so you fling it in the back of a cupboard never to trouble your earholes again.

Quite why the artist once celebrated for recording radio-friendly pop music thinks the world wants to listen as they thump a gong with a couple of pork chops is a mystery. But think it they do, and bang the gongs they will. Ours is neither to question, nor to listen, but simply to avoid.

Exercise

See if you can get a Mercury Music Prize nomination by recording your own world music album. Here's how to do it.

Step 1
Think of an instrument you can't play. Got one? Great – this is the instrument you will be playing on the album.

Step 2
Call Youssou N'Dour and see if he wants to make a world music album with you. If he doesn't, ask him for his cousin's phone number. Call Youssou N'Dour's cousin and ask him if he wants to make a world music album with you. If he doesn't, ask him for a friend's phone number. Repeat this process until somebody from Senegal agrees to record a world music album with you.

Step 3
Meet the person who has agreed to work with you and go to a quietish room. Turn on GarageBand and ask him to prattle on about a miscarriage of justice or a famous boat or something while you toot on or thump the instrument you can't play. Record for hours and hours.

Step 4

Photograph a crying child in black and white. This is your album cover. Package the audio mess inside this cover and send to Damon Albarn and BBC 6 Music.

Step 5

Sit back and wait for your Mercury Music Prize nomination. Attend the ceremony where you will lose out to a proper artist, make a fool of yourself in front of Radiohead and wish you were sat at a table with someone other than Youssou N'Dour, Youssou N'Dour's cousin or one of Youssou N'Dour's cousin's friends.

32

" Sorry. **"**

There are plenty of times when we say 'sorry' and it's not true because we don't really mean it, as in: 'Sorry, I can't come to your baby shower.' No one is sorry they can't go to a baby shower.

But more often than not we don't mean it when we say sorry, because we have nothing to actually be sorry for. Such as:

'Sorry!' – when someone has walked into YOU.

'Sorry, I only have a ten-pound note', 'Sorry, I've only got pound coins' or any situation where you feel you need to apologise for not having the correct change when paying for something.

'Sorry, this doesn't fit me.' It's okay, that's why the shop gave you a receipt in the first place. You are allowed to change things. It's not a big deal.

'Sorry, you're sitting in my seat.' Are you really apologising for someone else's mix-up?

'*Sorry, can I have another pint please?*' You're in a pub; they want you to drink.

'*Sorry?*' *accompanied with a pained face when someone has put their bag on the only free seat on the bus or train.* Why are you sorry that they are selfishly hogging a space?

'*Sorry, I'm not going to have a starter.*' That's OK. No one really needs a starter. The waiter doesn't care.

'*Sorry, I'm going to have to leave work at 6pm today.*' Which is when you're meant to leave.

'*Sorry, I think I've been shot.*' Not your fault. Unless you're a drug lord, in which case I doubt you won your tough-guy reputation by apologising all the time.

'*Sorry, is that the train to Dover?*' You're sorry that it might be the train to Dover?

'*Well, I'm sorry, but I disagree.*' Why are you sorry that you disagree? The other person is wrong.

'*Sorry, you're standing on my foot.*' I mean, really?

'*Sorry, can I just get through to get upstairs?*' when what you mean to say is: '*Why have you got on the bus and just huddled near the stairs when there's loads of room up top?! Now other people won't be let on the bus?!*'

106

'Sorry, will you marry me?' The words no girl wants to hear.

Exercises

1. Try and buy something in a newsagents without saying sorry.

2. 'Sorry seems to be the hardest word to say.' Or is it the easiest? Discuss.

3. Is it ever appropriate to say 'sorry' during the act of lovemaking? Show your workings.

LIE # 33

"*Just one more episode and then I'm off to bed.*"

In the old days, before DVD players and the internet, you could only watch your favourite programmes when they were broadcast on the actual telly. Miss them and they were gone forever, which is why episodes of *Bergerac* and *Brush Strokes* regularly drew audiences of 40 million. But then along came box sets, and it was suddenly possible to watch 500 episodes of *The West Wing* in one sitting. Box-set bingeing became a lifestyle choice and by the light of some cheese on toast we would happily watch *The Killing*, *The Bridge* and the whole of *The World at War* in one weekend. Now, with everything available in the gawp of an eye, the problem isn't choosing what to watch, but knowing when to stop, and that's why we find ourselves telling the 'just one more episode' lie.

For those of us with jobs to go to, 9 p.m. seems like a perfect time to be starting a new episode. By 10 p.m. you've seen Don Draper drink nine whiskies and take his trousers off twice. You should be relaxed and ready for bed. But the 10 p.m. finish is a dangerous one. It still seems a bit early to be sliding under the covers and you know you can squeeze one more in and still be in bed by 11 p.m. You notice that Huw Edwards has only just started reading the news and he must be, what, eighty years old? If an eighty-year-old is just starting work then you have no right to be going to bed. So you hit the next episode and watch Don Draper take his trousers off again. And now it's eleven.

Go to bed now and all is fine. You might be a tad bleary in the morning, but unless you're a milkman or training to be the heavyweight champion of the world you should be able to bag at least eight hours. But make the mistake of trying to sneak in one more episode and all is lost. If you're still viewing at midnight, a voice in your head will tell you you've already crossed a line, so why not cross it some more. And with each passing episode the series conclusion starts to slide into view. If you can just make it to 4 a.m. you'll be as up to date as it's possible to be and you can freely use Twitter without fear of spoilers. In fact, you can spoil it for others, and that's a seductive thought. And so on you go.

Around 3 a.m. you start to suffer from what's known as Box-Set Fear. As you slide the next disc into the DVD player you catch sight of yourself in the reflection of the TV screen and feel completely and utterly alone. You look gaunt and pale, frightened even. Your room as quiet as a cotton-wool church. Outside, frost creeps across the fields, birds sleep. More than ever you need the company of friends, and you find them in the shape of Don and Roger, Peggy and Joan.

By 6 a.m. you've finished the entire series. But you don't call it a series: you call it a season. A few years ago when friends of yours starting saying 'season' you wanted to punch them in the face. You despised their American pretensions. But now you say it all the time and it just sounds right. In fact, anyone who says 'series' must be an idiot. Or your mum. 'Have you been watching that new series with Robson Green?' she asks you on the phone. 'I love that series with Brenda Blethyn' it says on her T-shirt when you pick her up from the station.

These are the kind of startling insights you only ever have at 6 a.m. as you sit in your pants on the sofa, so you celebrate your genius with a fun-size Milky Way. Before long, morning is coughing at the window and the music looping on the DVD menu screen has lodged itself deep inside your tired mind. You quickly jump on the internet to see what others are saying about the season you've just completed and immediately find a link to the first eight episodes of the next one, which isn't out here until next year. You study your reflection in a spoon. Aside from being upside down you have bags under your eyes like shallow graves. And there's a lining on your teeth like the sort of things foals are wrapped in when they fall out of the big horse. It's time to tell the next lie in the 'just one more episode' sequence.

You open your email and start typing. 'Dear Mike' (95 per cent of bosses are called Mike). 'I've been up all night with some sort of bug thing and don't think I'm going to be able to make it in today. As much as anything I don't want to spread it around. Apologies for the inconvenience, but I think that a day in bed and a glug of Night Nurse should do the trick, and all being well I'll be back in bright and early tomorrow. Yours, Don Draper.'

And off it goes, with the plausibly ill-sounding sent time of 6.15 a.m. Mike will never suspect a thing.

Do you ever find yourself in that situation where you watch a show with your wife or partner?

Lee:

I have to do it with just one or the other. I'm not allowed to watch it at the same time with both.

But say you're watching something like *The Killing* **or** *Breaking Bad* **and you have to watch it together, but you want to get ahead and your partner isn't around—**

Lee:

You'll pretend you haven't seen it?

Yes, you'll sneak an episode without them.

Rob:

I've done that.

David:

Have you?

Rob:

Yes. [*Looks ashamed, clears throat.*] Hi, my name's Rob Brydon and I have cheated on my wife. But it was more of a fling really, I mean, I just watched about twenty minutes of *House of Cards* and then

I stopped. I didn't feel good about myself and I haven't ever told my wife, and I think it's a tribute to my acting skills that I was able to react to the unfolding events on the screen as if I'd never seen them before.

Silence as the earth-shattering nature of this claim fills the room. Only to be broken by . . .

Lee:
Permission to go to the toilet, sir.

He exits. David peels a clementine. Rob stares out of the window like a man staring out of a window.

"Doesn't the bride look beautiful!"

On average, people are average-looking. This stands to reason. Some are hot, some not. We can't all scrub up like Julie Christie, Julia Roberts or Johnny Depp. For every Christie there must be a Biggins.

Or at least you would think so. But no. Because apparently there is one day of the year when this doesn't apply. For on the day that two people get married it is compulsory to remark upon the beauty of the bride. Most of the time, it is a pleasure to do so: the bride is happy, her smile is radiant, her hair's well nice and she looks good enough to nibble.

But, you know, sometimes, just *sometimes*, no matter how much time, money and plastic surgery has gone into her appearance, she's just not cutting it. Not for you, not for anyone. Perhaps not even for the groom.

Beauty is subjective and comparative. Perhaps you think she's beautiful, even if no one else does. Perhaps she's beautiful *compared* to what she normally looks like (a hyena). In that case everyone can say how beautiful she looks and not feel like they are lying because she does look a hell of a lot better than the last time she got married.

Unfortunately, the requirement to comment upon the bride's good looks is overriding to the extent that it rarely comes out naturally. Many a best man has uttered the line 'And doesn't the bride look beautiful?' so robotically as to render her feeling as pretty as a pig. Occasionally, though, he means it. A tear may prick his eye; he may cast a longing look her way and remember that one night of magic last July when her fiancé was attending the regional sales conference in Swanage.

So should we do it? Hell, yep. On a day celebrating love and joy anything else comes across as sour grapes. Only a sociopath, former lover or catty bachelor would feel the need to put the bride's looks down on her wedding day. Unfortunately, that makes up 46 per cent of the congregation.

> 'She looks like a skeleton.'
> 'She's drunk and her eyes are puffy.'
> 'Isn't she *ugly* when she smiles?'
> 'Cream isn't her colour.'
> 'I've seen that dress online for £17.'

Complimenting the bride's looks is just one of many social conventions we must force ourselves through on a wedding day. Others include telling the parents 'you must be very proud' even though their son's just been released from prison; wishing the newlyweds a 'a future of happiness' despite them screwing you over in a business venture; and squeezing the hand of your partner during the ceremony while you scheme your way out of the relationship. No wonder everyone gets drunk.

But we are right to compliment the bride. The gap in her front teeth has been filled with a combination of polyfiller and toothpaste, she's shaved her monobrow into two clearly delineated eyebrows and she's lost six stone. Most of all, through the beard, she looks happy.

LIE # 35

"I've left my wallet at home."

You don't like spending money. Your father didn't like spending money and nor did his father, or his father before him. Or your mum. Or sister. Frankly no one in your family likes spending money. It's amazing you're even dressed.

But you are and you're in the pub. You hate the pub. You like drinking but hate paying. It's not an attractive quality of yours. Alongside eating your own earwax it's your least appealing trait. But you can only be yourself and that's what makes you lovable.

Your wallet's about your person but is hidden in a secure lining that requires a three-digit combination and fingerprint ID to access. Will you be taking it out? No chance. You appreciate too much the aesthetics of money, especially notes, and hate to see them broken down into smaller denominations.

'Whose round is it anyway?' goes the cry. You feign a full body check before declaring that you have forgotten your wallet. Groans ensue. These people know you.

'Tell you what, I'll lend you a score,' says some idiot.

117

Oh dear. This is bad. In fact it's the worst-case scenario. All you're after is a few free drinks and an early night.

'Here you go, mate.'

They thrust a £20 note into your midriff.

'Balls,' says your head.

'Pay us back next time.'

You feel extremely unhappy and briefly consider moving to South America. Slowly your brain cranks into action. How to get out of this situation? 'Next time . . . next time . . .' The words echo round your head. Then it dawns on you. There won't *be* a next time! You decide there and then that this shall be your swansong with this particular group of gents.

'Who's having what?' you say, feeling unbelievably generous. 'My shout. Whatever you fancy. Up to the value of £2.30.'

Someone asks for a pint of lager *and* a packet of crisps. Inside you're dying, but you push through the pain. As you do you recall with great fondness the dinner for Lauren's thirtieth. Such a lavish affair! Eighteen bottles of champagne (you drank six), caviar, fancy fish, luscious veg and cake all round. Only when you nipped to the loo, they split the bill. On your return someone asked you to stump up £351. You coughed so loudly children were woken in Scunthorpe.

'What do you think about doing a runner?' you suggested politely to the birthday girl. She looked back at you with disdain. Probably for the best, your knee had given out the previous week legging it from Dr Hunger's all-you-can-eat buffet.

Then it came to you: 'Terribly sorry,' you said. 'Left my blasted wallet at home.' Everyone stared at you, incredulous, but you didn't care. You'd won. David Aldrich covered you and you immediately made a point of never seeing him again. When Susan Hammond emailed you on David's behalf you got your mum to say you'd died and left nothing behind except best wishes.

Back in the pub you pay for a full round. It feels scary handing over £20 until you remember it's not your money. A sense of warmth envelops your being.

'This is counterfeit!' screams the bar lady, the note raised in her bird-like hand. You look at her. Then you look behind at your mates, but all you see is a swinging door.

'But I don't . . .'

'Pay up now, turnip-face, or I'm calling the fuzz!'

Reluctantly, you fumble inside your jacket and type in the three-digit code.

LIE # 36

"Another winner!" – David Manning, *The Ridgefield Press*.
And other movie quote lies

You're probably wise to the practice of plucking a few choice words from an unfavourable film review and quoting them entirely out of context.

(For example, when New Line Cinema quoted critic Owen Gleiberman's review on the poster for the Brad Pitt thriller *SE7EN*, they put the words 'a small masterpiece'. But in the actual review Gleiberman only said that about the film's opening titles.)

But in 2001, Sony Pictures Entertainment went one step further than just picking out the words they liked from a review – they made up the review itself. And then invented the critic who supposedly wrote it.

His name was David Manning, and he worked for *The Ridgefield Press*, a small weekly newspaper in Connecticut. Except he didn't exist.

But that didn't stop his quotes appearing on the posters for movies by Sony Pictures. Health Ledger, star of *A Knight's Tale*, was described by David Manning as 'This year's hottest star!' and maybe he was, even if David

Manning was just a figment of Sony's marketing department.

But people began to question Manning's judgement when he described the Rob Schneider flop *The Animal* as 'Another winner!' as if Schneider had ever had a previous hit film.

And when he described the Kevin Bacon sci-fi turkey *Hollowman* as 'one hell of a scary ride' it was only a matter of time before the truth came out.

When *Newsweek* reporter John Horn – a real journalist who actually worked for a publication – began to investigate David Manning, he revealed that *The Ridgefield Press* – a real paper – had never heard of Manning.

In an out of court settlement Sony agreed to pay $5 to moviegoers that had seen one of its films on the basis of Manning's reviews. But is that enough to make anyone own up to seeing a Rob Schneider film?

Exercise

1. Type your own review of this book, then get rid of any negative words, take out the positive ones and write them in crayon on the front cover. Congratulations, you are a book reviewer.

LIE # 37

"Come on in, it's not cold!"

Every day around the coast of Britain you can hear this lie blurted from the mouth of a breathless idiot shambling about in the dirty brown sea. 'Come on in, it's not cold!' they say, as you stare in disbelief from the wind-lashed shore. Even when the sun melts the tarmac, and dogs gasp for air in the backs of boiling cars, the sea in these parts is the temperature of death. If you want to know what it feels like to be molested by a snowman, come on in.

For some reason, jumping into any body of freezing cold water is considered a worthy thing to do. Be it a river, the sea, a stream, a pond or a lido, submitting your epidermis to the swirling chill is the mark of a superior human. It's a demonstration of strength and a confirmation of your oneness with nature. Why this should be is unclear: it hurts and you don't need to do it. Nobody expects the respect of their peers for smashing their hand with a lump hammer, yet leap in a lake on Christmas Eve and adoring eyes will watch you dry.

'Come on in, it's not cold!' is disingenuous on a number of levels. Firstly it *is* cold. That we've already established. Secondly, they don't really want you to join them. That would undermine their prowess. One man in the sea on his own is an adventurer searching for the meaning of life. Two are just mucking about. Thirdly, the whole lie is actually for the benefit of others beyond the immediate party shivering on the shingle. What the fool is really shouting through their stupid chattering teeth is: 'Hey, you! You over there walking your dog. Look at me, I'm in the sea. In November! I know, mad isn't it? But that's just me. I'm a free spirit, a maverick, a risk-taker. Society can't contain my impulses. And look at my square friends, all wrapped up in their scarves and coats. They're pathetic conformists, terrified to challenge themselves, let alone take on the world. They don't have my lust for life, and neither, I expect, do you. I mean look at us. I'm in the sea in November and you're pacing along the beach in the wind stooping to scoop your dog's bum plums into a polythene bag. You're a cog in the system, just like everybody else. I despise you and everything you represent. But while I've got your attention, can I borrow a towel?'

Often, the cold sea swimmer does it for the benefit of a girl. But unless she's a complete idiot, this is ill-advised. The smart girl doesn't see an act of manliness, she sees a spluttering, goose-bumped idiot flounder in the surf with a used condom on his head. And the post-swim tiptoed jig across the stones, as if walking on upturned plugs, does little to improve perceptions.

123

If anybody ever says this lie to you, see it clearly for what it is: an act of grand vanity. Button your coat, bury your hands deep in your pockets and head for the light of the tavern. For there, by the glow of the fire, the mysteries of life are all within your grasp. Come on in, it really isn't cold.

38

> " It's Friday afternoon, let's do this meeting in the pub. I honestly think " we'll get more done over a beer.

So, look, I've got an idea.

I know we've still got to work out what we do about that thing. No, not that thing, the other thing. We can leave that thing till Monday. We need to think about the first thing now. There's quite a lot of stuff to work out about it.

But I've been thinking. You know, most people in the office are still pretty whacked from doing that big thing yesterday, but now we've got the Bendix Report off, I have a feeling that some people aren't really concentrating. They're just focusing on the weekend, and Facebook pictures, and thinking about what it would be like if they got off with each other and then dismissing that idea. By the way, didn't Madeline do a really good job on the Bendix Report? She chose a really good font for the front and was totally across the binding process.

So. We could get everyone into a meeting room – you, me, Madeline, the others – and really drive them for a couple of hours and hopefully sort it out.

But, I'm not sure that everyone would be at the top of their game, things might come out a bit fuzzy and we'd have to go through it all again on Monday morning. And besides which, and this isn't that important obviously, it might not be very good for morale to sit everyone in a grey old meeting room on a nice afternoon like this. I have a feeling that everyone will just sit fiddling on their phones all the time. And begin to hate you. And me.

But, I've had an idea. It might sound a bit counterintuitive but I think it could really work.

It's Friday afternoon: let's do this meeting in the pub, I honestly think we'll get more done over a beer.

Yeah? Whaddya think? Sounds fun? *And* productive?

Let's you, me, Madeline, the other guys, all go to the pub. People will relax a bit with a drink in their hand. And they'll focus on the job more, especially if the music isn't too loud. People will want to get it done quickly so that they can concentrate on going home or going out or thinking about getting off with each other. I honestly think we'll get more work done, quicker, in the pub than in an office specifically designed for getting work done. I know, sounds weird, but that's what I think.

I'll take all the bits of paper with me. And I'll take notes. On my phone. And if we need to look anything up, I can do that on my phone as well. I'll take a charger just in case. We'll get a table near a socket. And even if the battery runs out I can make notes on serviettes with a pen borrowed from the bar.

I think a lot of the team – especially Madeline – would really appreciate a change of scene. We may get to see a different side of them. Especially after three or four large glasses of wine.

I honestly think we would get more done.

Exercise

1. What time of day did I write this? Show your working. Even if you're working in a pub.

LIE # 39

" Giving birth really isn't as bad as people say it is. "

It is. In fact, it's much worse, but the laws of nature dictate that no woman can ever tell another exactly how horrific it is. If they did, the human race would cease to exist. And that's bad for business.

Now, why not use the rest of this page to jot down your favourite baby names. Happy thinking!

Do you think there is an unspoken contract between women that they will never tell another woman how painful giving birth really is?

Rob:

No, I think what it is – and I find it amazing – is that they forget the . . . discomfort. Let's not use the word 'pain'.

Lee:

Yeah, but never mind the way she got pregnant, Rob, stick to the question.

LIE # 40

"It wasn't me."

You are ten. You are in a room on your own. Also in the room is a fragile object. Let's say it's a vase. You are aware that this vase is very breakable. Very, very breakable. You are aware that the slightest knock will upset it from its place and it will smash into a thousand pieces. In fact, beyond this, an adult has pointed out the vase to you, and made special reference to quite how delicate it is. You must be very, very careful not to touch the vase.

You decide to bounce your tennis ball against the wall.

This might seem dangerous, foolhardy perhaps. But it's OK, because you're going to throw the tennis ball against the exact opposite wall from where the vase is. So it's all going to be OK. You will be doubly careful not to upset the vase. So there's not going to be any problems. But to be extra sure, you will take it one bounce at a time for the first few.

Bounce. Catch.

That went well. No problem at all. Easy. The vase is still on the shelf.

Bounce. Catch.

Another good one. Vase still absolutely intact.

Bounce. Catch. Bounce. Catch. Bounce. Catch. Bounce. Catch. Bounce. Catch. Bounce. Catch. Bounce. Catch. Bounce. Catch. Bounce. Catch. Bounce. Catch. Bounce. Catch. Bounce. Catch.

Vase still absolutely intact. There is absolutely no danger.

Bounce. Catch. Bounce. Catch. Bounce. Catch. Bounce. Catch. Bounce. Catch. Bounce. Catch. Bounce. Catch. Bounce. Catch. Bounce. Catch. Bounce. Catch. Bounce. Catch. Bounce. Catch.

The vase is still intact. It's probably not as fragile as it looks. Because it looks really fragile, and if it was as fragile as it looks it would simply fall apart when a piece of dust fell on it.

Bounce. Catch. Bounce. Catch. Bounce. Catch. Bounce. Catch. Bounce. Catch. Bounce. Catch. Bounce. Catch. Bounce. Catch. Bounce. Catch. Bounce. Catch. Bounce. Catch. Bounce. Catch.

Still fine. You have a thought. An interesting thought. How close to the vase can you bounce the ball *without* breaking the vase?

There's only one way to find out.

Bounce. Catch. Bounce. Catch. Bounce. Catch. Bounce. Catch. Bounce. Catch. Bounce. Catch. Bounce. Catch. Bounce. Catch. Bounce. Catch. Bounce. Catch. Bounce. Catch. Bounce. Catch.

Edging ever closer. Still the vase is OK. Maybe the vase is sturdier than you think.

Bounce. Catch. Bounce. Catch. Bounce. Catch. Bounce. Catch. Bounce. Catch. Bounce. Catch. Bounce. Catch. Bounce. Catch. Bounce. Catch. Bounce. Catch. Bounce. Catch. Bounce. *Crash!*

The vase is now on the floor. In pieces. It is no longer a vase. It is just some bits of stuff. Something to fill a dustpan and brush with.

Could you put it together again?

But you don't have a chance to continue this thought, because the sound of it smashing has brought every adult in the house into the room.

And there they see you, your ball and the smashed vase.

Before you have had time to think of the best thing to say, your mouth has started moving. And the lie it tells is one that's been told since the dawn of time: 'It wasn't me.'

LIE # 41

"I don't want to talk about it."

When somebody says they don't want to talk about it they are usually desperate to talk about it. Whatever 'it' happens to be. If they weren't, they wouldn't do that thing where they walk into the office or throw themselves down on the sofa and audibly harrumph until somebody asks them if something is wrong. This is their cue to say that nothing is wrong, before waiting a moment and then making the harrumphing noise again. If this particular harrumph is ignored they will usually make a third one, slightly changing the tone and volume of the harrumph to ensure that the other person asks the question again. Only this time they don't say that nothing is wrong, but offer the much more intriguing: 'I don't want to talk about it.' This is a downright lie. All they want to do is talk about it. In fact all they've been thinking about for the past hour is how the minute they see you they are going to make a harrumphing noise until you ask them what's wrong and they can tell you all about it. Usually while drinking three bottles of wine and smoking forty cigarettes.

How it plays out from here is very much dependent on the interrogator. Respect a person's wish to not want to talk about it and the loop starts again, but with the harrumph being replaced by a very deep sigh or moan. Fail to question these new signals and the person who really wants to talk about it will throw something across the room in an escalating attempt to reel you in. It might be a stapler or TV remote, but never the towel. These people never give in.

More often than not the 'it' is a boyfriend or girlfriend; sometimes it's a parent, or sibling. Rarely is it anything you have the remotest interest in or that you haven't heard before. In fact, in most cases, it's something you thought you'd made very clear you weren't at all interested in the last time you spoke about it following a protracted bout of harrumphing and throwing things.

The only redeeming feature of this situation is the wine. They need it to keep their tongue loose; you need it to blank out the fact that you're listening to them dribble on about something of such monumental insignificance. If it wasn't for the wine this situation couldn't sustain. Within minutes you'd be screaming at them to go and find someone who really cares that she doesn't love you any more, or that he's been seeing someone else, or that so and so stole your idea at work and passed it off as their own. But with the Pinot Grigio to hand it's perfectly possible to nod in the right places and make the right noises without listening to a single word they say. Their bottom lip may wobble and their eyes may mist, but your mind is free to wander and consider more interesting things. Like is John Nettles on Twitter and how do zips work?

The next time a friend gives you the opening har-rumph, harrumph right back. It's a bold move, but as long as you can stick to it you can echo their game plan every step of the way. Before you know it, the two of you are locked in an unbreakable standoff, the only solution to which is to open a bottle of wine and say absolutely nothing. And should they ever dare to break the silence and ask you what's wrong, just toe the party line and tell them in no uncertain terms that you really, really don't want to talk about it.

LIE # 42

"I'll *take a look* at the dessert menu."

Why is this a lie? Because it's only said when people already know that they don't want a dessert. Why don't people just say, 'I don't want a dessert, thanks'? Do they think they are breaking the heart of the waitress? Why do they want the waitress to think that there's a possibility they might have a dessert? The waitress *knows* that you are not going to have a dessert. How does she know? Because when asked, 'Would you like to see the dessert menu?' someone who actually wants a dessert just says 'Yes'. Only someone who doesn't actually want a dessert says, '*I'll take a look*.'

It's the strange way they say, '*I'll take a look*' that is weird, like a little girl doing dolly voices. The inference is this: 'I don't want a dessert because I'm too full up/ watching my weight/should be going/don't like the person I'm having dinner with/don't even like desserts, BUT there might be something on the dessert menu so utterly *sensational* that it will overcome all of those factors and basically force its way into my stomach. But *I very much* doubt that that will happen, ha ha!'

Just imagine all the time that could be saved in restaurants if people who didn't want a dessert stopped saying '*I'll take a look*' and just said 'No, thanks' instead. All that time that could be freed up for the waiters and waitresses to, you know, just smile at the customers and think about all the free puddings they can eat when their shift ends. All that time they wouldn't have to spend traipsing through the restaurant getting a dessert menu for someone who doesn't want a dessert, then, once that person has admitted they don't want a dessert, taking that dessert menu from the table and retracing their steps to put it back where it belongs. All that time, utterly wasted, because, for some reason, people don't want the waitress to know that they don't actually want a dessert.

Exercises

1. Go for dinner. Have a dessert.

2. Go for dinner. Say: 'No, I don't need to see the dessert menu, I'm not, and this is obvious to me at this point, going to have a dessert, so please save yourself the bother of getting the menu and use the time instead to plot your revenge on all the other diners who have unnecessarily wasted your time and shoe leather asking for one when they have no intention of ordering.'

LIE # 43

"I think *Citizen Kane* is the greatest movie ever made."

Anybody who ever says this sentence is either in an interview for film school, on a first date, the editor of *Sight and Sound* or somebody at a dinner party at the editor of *Sight and Sound*'s house. More often than not they haven't even seen *Citizen Kane*, they've just read in *Empire* magazine that it's supposed to be good or overheard Melvin Bragg in a Hampstead café trotting out the platitude to a sycophantic journalist. *Citizen Kane* is *fine*. But that's all. It's shot nicely and it tells a story. But it's also pretty dull. Two hours of dull in deep focus.

If Channel 4 ever make any more of those interminable list shows where they count down the top one hundred things from a bigger group of things (hats, moustaches, objects that really show up finger marks) they could do one for films that are 'fine' and *Citizen Kane* would rightly vie for the top spot. But the greatest movie ever made? Not even close.

We all know that *Raiders of the Lost Ark* is better than *Citizen Kane*, as is *Taxi Driver* and *The Godfather*. But it's not even as good as *The 'Burbs*. Or *Beverley Hills Cop*. Or

Freddy Got Fingered. Honestly, watch *Citizen Kane* and *Freddy Got Fingered* back to back and ask yourself which one you liked best. It won't be the boring old black-and-white one.

Anybody who says that *Citizen Kane* is the greatest movie ever made is lying to you and lying to themselves. And if you don't believe me, here's the proof.

Citizen Kane is not as good as *Turner and Hooch*.
Citizen Kane is not as good as *Free Willy*.
Citizen Kane is not as good as *Escape To Victory*.
Citizen Kane is not as good as *Throw Mamma from the Train*.
Citizen Kane is not as good as *Under Siege*.
Citizen Kane is not as good as *The Mummy*.
Citizen Kane is not as good as *Happy Gilmore*.
Citizen Kane is not as good as *Basil the Great Mouse Detective*.
Citizen Kane is not as good as *Jagged Edge*.
Citizen Kane is not as good as *Breakdance: The Movie*.
Citizen Kane is not as good as *Breakdance 2: Electric Boogaloo*.
Citizen Kane is not as good as *Caddyshack*.
Citizen Kane is not as good as *The Golden Child*.
Citizen Kane is not as good as *Space Jam*.
Citizen Kane is not as good as *Big Trouble in Little China*.
Citizen Kane is not as good as *Every Which Way But Loose*.
Citizen Kane is not as good as *Top Secret*.
Citizen Kane is not as good as *Snakes on a Plane*.
Citizen Kane is not as good as *Tango and Cash*.
Citizen Kane is not as good as *Three Men and a Little Lady*.

139

Citizen Kane is not as good as *Clockwise.*

Citizen Kane is not as good as *Carry On . . . Up the Khyber.*

Citizen Kane is not as good as *Bill & Ted's Bogus Journey.*

Citizen Kane is not as good as *Cocktail.*

Citizen Kane is not as good as *Presumed Innocent.*

Citizen Kane is not as good as *Herbie Goes Bananas.*

Citizen Kane is not as good as *The Karate Kid.*

Citizen Kane is not as good as *Tootsie.*

Citizen Kane is not as good as *Uncle Buck.*

Citizen Kane is not as good as *Tron.*

Citizen Kane is not as good as *Police Academy 3: Back in Training.*

Citizen Kane is not as good as *Freaky Friday.*

Citizen Kane is not as good as *Parenthood.*

Citizen Kane is not as good as *Nuns on the Run.*

Citizen Kane is not as good as *Peter's Friends.*

Citizen Kane is not as good as *Arachnophobia.*

Citizen Kane is not as good as *Coyote Ugly.*

Citizen Kane is not as good as *Howard the Duck.*

Citizen Kane is not as good as *Bend It Like Beckham.*

Citizen Kane is not as good as *Sleuth.*

Citizen Kane is not as good as *The Business.*

Citizen Kane is not as good as *When Saturday Comes.*

Citizen Kane is not as good as *The Rock.*

Citizen Kane is not as good as *Bad Boys.*

Citizen Kane is not as good as *Short Circuit.*

Citizen Kane is not as good as *Digby, the Biggest Dog in the World.*

Citizen Kane is not as good as *Anaconda.*

Citizen Kane is not as good as *The Boy in the Plastic Bubble.*

Citizen Kane is not as good as *Johnny English*.
Citizen Kane is not as good as *One of Our Dinosaurs is Missing*.

I could go on.

LIE # 44

"*Have a nice day.*"

It was our friends across the pond who first introduced us to the pleasures of 'have a nice day'. Of course everything American eventually makes its way to these shores (the hamburger, the motorcar, Gwyneth Paltrow). Today bank clerks and baristas up and down the land are forced to mimic this most unfortunate of phrases. Asking the English to sincerely wish anyone a nice day runs contrary to our suspicious, small island mentality. If we say it we rarely mean it.

'That'll be £17.30,' you tell the lady dressed head-to-toe in Versace. Her face betrays the signs of botox. She is on the phone.

'Ya,' she says into the receiver. 'Oh ya. Of course I'll be there dahling. I wouldn't miss a Sotheby's champagne night for the world!'

'Would you like cashback?' you ask.

'Hold on dahling,' she says down the line. 'Checkout girl's talking to me. Poor little thing doesn't know any better . . .'

'Cashback?' you say again.

'£8,000 please.'

'I can only give you fifty.'

'That'll have to do I suppose,' she says fixing you with a glare.

A warm feeling reaches the pit of your stomach as you picture the woman falling from a cliff top and landing on a spike, before being eaten to death by an ant that resembles Tony Blair.

Suddenly her face turns ashen.

'Oh my god!' she says. 'Ohmygod ohmygod ohmygod! I forgot the chocolate Bath Olivers! Wait there and don't serve anyone else.'

The woman disappears. The rest of the queue stares at you. You force a smile. Seven minutes pass. Two people leave. Eventually she returns with six Jerusalem artichokes, two packets of gravlax, a pound of kosher bacon and a parrot.

'This shop is extremely badly organised,' she says. 'Literally no one seems to know where the anchovy paste is. I demand to speak with the manager.'

You drift off again, picturing her strapped to a railway track, getting sliced in two then being feasted upon by walking sharks.

'I can arrange that for you madam,' you reply politely.

'Honestly this is the last time I allow Consuela to abandon us,' she says. 'I shall never enter a supermarket again. It is beneath me.'

You count out the money and return her card.

'I'm going to write to my local MP,' she continues. 'I know him personally so expect repercussions. You people don't know the first thing about service. Twice this year there's not even been the hint of a quail's egg. Richard can't eat normal eggs, not since the accident. How do you expect to maintain custom with such irregularity? This is the worst experience of my life, and that includes a simply agonising trip to Selfridges in 1988. Don't think for a moment you'll be getting off scot free either young lady.'

'Have a nice day,' you say, picturing the woman being crushed by a falling Volvo.

'And you,' she replies.

LIE # 45

"What a beautiful baby!"

We were all babies once, and some of us are pretty ugly, so it stands to reason that some of us were ugly babies. That's just maths. Or biology. Yet on seeing a baby for the very first time almost everybody will describe it as beautiful, regardless of its visage. We just can't tell a mother who has been through the pain of childbirth that her son looks like a deflating balloon, or that her daughter has the grimace of a strangler's mugshot.

Often, the first time we set eyes on the hideous creature is in the company of others. A mother brings the baby into the office and parades it around near the photocopier like a football manager with the FA Cup. People leap from their desks (any excuse to get a break from the admin of capitalism) and stand in horseshoe formation to clap eyes on the thing that was previously just a lump under the jumper. She lifts the bundle from the pram and twists its contorted face towards the assembled throng, and suddenly everyone is looking for an excuse to return to the admin of capitalism. A Mexican wave of awkward looks plays across the faces of the onlookers, as before

145

them a squashed conker with fists for eyes dribbles breast gloop onto a franking machine. Eventually somebody steps forward with a nurturing caress and breaks the silence. 'What a beauty!' they say. 'Absolutely gorgeous!' And suddenly the rest of the group is granted the freedom to make other observations. Things like: 'He's definitely got your eyes.' 'Hasn't she got big hands!' and 'Did you know that Janice has taken your parking space?'

As parents we are unable to see our own children as anything other than beautiful. This is a good thing. It means that we continue to feed them, and don't get frightened in the night when their googly eyes spy at us from the hollow of the Moses basket. And it's this belief in our own offspring's perfectness that allows the lie to go unnoticed. Wherever they go, new parents hear people telling them that their baby is beautiful, and they believe it to be true. And here's the really interesting thing: it actually is true.

This may be the only example in this book of a line we all say, thinking it to be a lie, when we are unwittingly speaking the truth. All babies *are* beautiful. Each and every one of them is a completely unique ball of human potential, the product of millions and millions of years of chaotic evolution, as wondrous, complex and unfathomable as the universe itself. Each and every baby is a work of art; each and every baby is a poem. Yes, some of them might not conform to an ad-man's notion of physical perfection, but who gives a soiled nappy about that? So what if she looks like a tiny Walter Matthau; so what if he looks like an angry onion. You don't own the definition of what is beautiful and neither do I.

'What a beautiful baby!' you lie, and all anybody hears is the undisputed truth.

On seeing a new baby people will always say, 'Oh, isn't he or she beautiful!' but they may not really think that at all.

Lee:

Yeah, 90 per cent of babies you see you neither think are beautiful or ugly. You just think that's a baby.

Rob:

But now and again one does come along that's an absolute shocker and you think, oh my God—

Lee:

—I better have another one.

Rob:

Ha!

Lee:

The amount of children you have definitely relates to how attractive the first one is.

Rob:

That's why I've had five children. I just keep going hoping that one of them is going to pass the beauty test.

Lee:

You're the eldest of fifteen aren't you?

Rob:

[*Laughs*] Yes, which gives you some idea of what my

parents were dealing with. If they were happy with this, imagine what the others were like.

Lee:

I find it's not so much the look as the size of the head. I don't think I've seen an attractive baby with a massive head.

Rob:

And if the mother is there when you're meeting the baby with the massive head you can only be thinking about one thing and she knows you're thinking it.

Lee:

Yes, and it's hard for me because I'm very naive about how the whole thing works and how it got in there in the first place. Often I'm thinking – that's a big head, how did it get up there? And sometimes I'll even ask the mother, which I can tell you is a mistake.

LIE # 46

" I haven't revised. **"**

You are standing outside the examination room, desperately cramming last-minute facts (Magna Carta 1215/Prohibition 1920/Gazza 1990). You're in a panic because you haven't done enough. It's all been rather last minute. It always is with you. Frankly, you're a bit of a disaster. The last thing you need right now is Simon Felcher appearing at your shoulder.

'Oh God, I haven't done *any* revision,' says Felcher, the brightest boy in the year. 'I'm probably going to fail. In fact I *know* I am. My life is effectively over.'

Is Felcher deliberately trying to make you feel inadequate or is it subconscious? Does he believe his own words or is this merely a charade he must perform in order to settle himself down? Who knows, perhaps he *hasn't* revised. Either way you are sure of two things: Simon Felcher will score a straight A, while you'll be pleased if you scrape a D (especially as Miss Eames predicts an E).

Foolishly, you seek to question the limitations of Felcher's knowledge, while simultaneously displaying your own.

'Did you read anything about what happened *after* the Wars of the Roses ended in 1495?' you proffer.

'They ended in 1485 not 1495 you *turnip*,' replies Simon. 'Anyway I know all *that*. That's *basic* stuff. I read about it in my *spare time*.'

His *spare time*? In your spare time you sit by the big tree outside Boots and drink budget cider. Thankfully, you are too young and innocent to consider the reality of Simon Felcher's peculiarly isolated and sad existence, and begin looking at your revision cards again.

A minute later, as you scan the life of Henry VII, you realise how utterly inadequate Felcher makes you feel. The fury rises within you. You are livid. You confront Felcher.

'You always *claim* you haven't revised,' you say, barely able to contain your anger, 'yet you always get amazing grades.'

'Maybe, but this time I really haven't done *anything*,' counters Felcher, silencing you once more.

If we inform those around us that we haven't prepared for an event (exam/dinner party/World Cup final) it lowers the expectations both of ourselves and of others. This reduces the pressure we experience, freeing us up to relax and use our brains more efficiently. A brain feeling the strain tenses up, shrinks to one-eighth of its normal size and hides in the corner of the skull.

The alternative to lowering expectations is to relax the brain through the power of alcohol. This explains why

97 per cent of dinner party hosts get drunk, and 63 per cent of all marathon runners. Drinking during exams is not permitted, however, except in Ireland.

But help is at hand. It's not just Simon Felcher who claims not to have done any work. Susan Boof appears from nowhere, her tie loose, skirt illegal, stinking of cognac. When Susan says she hasn't done any revision she means it.

'What's the point?' she says, 'Never going to pass sums anyway.'

'This isn't maths, it's history,' you reply.

'History?' she says.

'Yes.'

She pauses.

'Never gonna pass that neither.'

47

" I'm going to get Sky TV for Sky Arts. "

Ruddy Murdoch. You're never going to give in to him.

First he tried it with the football. And yes, it would be great to be able to watch the Premier League on your own sofa for a change rather than have to traipse off down the pub. You'd probably save money in the long run, the price of a pint these days. But the atmosphere is great down the pub, and there's always the FA Cup and the Champions League and anyway, you're not going to give Murdoch any of your money.

Then he tried it with the movies. Twelve channels of the latest blockbuster hits. Always a movie to watch. You love the movies. Movies, movies, movies. Maybe all those movies are going to make you sign up to Sky? Let's just have a look at the listings. No, no this isn't your sort of thing at all. *Jennifer's Body*? *You, Me and Dupree* on three times a day? No. Where's the latest Mike Leigh? Where's something in Japanese? No, you'll stick with Film4 on the old Freeview thanks. Don't want one of those ghastly squariels glued to the spare-room window just to see *Ghostbusters II* whenever you want. What would people think?

Murdoch hasn't got any of your money yet. Hang on – what's this in the TV listings pages? Sky Arts? That sounds like your sort of thing. Arts. You think you like Arts. Sounds like the sort of thing that people like you get into, Arts. Arty stuff. Things about . . . paintings and opera and theatre, and whatever else Arts is about. That sounds worth getting. Educational, cultural – worth getting a man around to plug it all in.

And so you get it. You get Sky TV for Sky Arts. And Sky Arts 2. In HD.

Murdoch may have taken your money, but you will have the last laugh. You will have expanded your mind so much that it will be worth it. It will be like having a library on tap. It's the TV equivalent of living in the British Museum.

When you sign up for it you think, well, it's only a little more to get the football and the movies, so you might as well. There might be the odd game you'll watch when you're not watching Sky Arts, or, on those very rare occasions when you want to take a break from Sky Arts 2, there might be a foreign-language film you can unwind with.

So, now you've got the full Sky package and you're very happy with it. You're not watching Sky Arts as much as you thought you might be. It turns out that most of the shows aren't really your cup of tea – old interviews with Johnny Cash and the Grateful Dead in concert in 1976 – but there are so many other channels to choose from. In fact, you never watch Sky Arts at all.

But as you settle in to watch Stoke City take on Watford on a Tuesday night, while recording the fourth Bourne film, it's comforting to think that you could watch Sky Arts whenever you feel like it.

And Murdoch hasn't won . . .

LIE # 48

66 I'm still at the office. 99

The phrase 'I'm still at the office' is as sure a sign your partner is having an affair as suddenly wearing aftershave to work or holding hands with another woman on the train. Sometimes the claim is genuine, they are still at the office, it's just that they have taken their trousers off and are canoodling with a colleague in the disabled toilets. Sometimes the claim is a lie, and they're in a country pub in the middle of nowhere kissing someone who tastes of wine, surrounded by other couples who have also told the office lie. (Why don't these country pubs with big car parks just come clean about their reason for existence and change their names to 'The Royal Infidelity', 'The Mucky Fumble' or 'The Don't Forget To Wash It'?)

Offices and affairs go together like tears and marriage guidance sessions. From nine to five, people button their collars and polish their shoes to play at being grown-ups amongst the hierarchies and power relationships that commerce demands. It's corporate S&M in a neutral space far removed from the jam handprints of the family home. We feign interest and nod at the PowerPoint while imagining each other undressed. We freshen our breath and play footsie under the table. We flirt on email and brush hands as we reach for the stapler. Day in, day out, we repeat the corporate courtship until a glass of Pinot while waiting for the train tips us over the edge and into the arms of another. Offices are undeniably *the* hot bed (or desk) of marital unfaithfulness.

In a pre-digital world it was a lot easier to phone the 'I'm still at the office' lie through to a partner and then get on with the business of tickling a co-worker's bottom. But in this super-connected world the deceit is a lot more complicated. Forget to change the settings on your phone and you can unwittingly announce to the world that at 9 p.m. you were enjoying a frottage by the bins of a French bistro. My advice to everyone is to always disable the 'Philanderer Mode' on any new phone. What do you mean you've not seen that before? It's in settings, just beneath the 'Gullibility' switch.

Of course, the liar who says that they are still in the office isn't always having a dalliance. Sometimes they just want to kick back with the girls or talk about snooker with the boys. Sometimes, a family man, fed up with trying to dodge the roller skates in the hall, just wants to sit by a quiet photocopier after hours and eat an orange without being disturbed.

Should you be worried if you are the recipient of the 'I'm still at the office' call? Of course not. Your relationship is solid, isn't it? You're together for ever, aren't you? Sure, you've not had much physical contact for a while, but that's only natural. You're both busy people. So what if neither of you makes that much of an effort any more, you don't need to, you're soul mates. You are soul mates who love nothing more than sitting side by side on a Saturday night and laughing and laughing at a Michael Macintyre DVD, and there's no better feeling in the world than that. Ha ha ha ha ha ha ha! Ha ha ha ha ha ha ha! You've got nothing in the world to worry about. Just keep on laughing. They'll be home soon.

LIE # 49

"We'll finish your bathroom on Monday."

'We'll finish your bathroom on Monday,' say the builders. And that would be great. Except that's what they said last week. And the week before that. And the week before that.

You haven't seen them, in the flesh, for weeks. They were there all the time when they first started. Really getting down to it. Looked like it was going to be finished way ahead of schedule. And then one day, they just stopped coming.

At first you thought it was just a one-off thing. Maybe they were all ill. All of them? What were their names again? Nice guys.

But then they didn't turn up the next day. A call would have been nice. Just to let you know. Eventually you call them.

Waiting on parts seems to be the thing. Have to be shipped from Italy or somewhere. Special parts. They should turn up soon. They don't have another more lucrative job somewhere else. No, they're just waiting on parts.

And they do turn up again. For half an hour. Then they seem to go again. Leaving the bathroom the same as it was before, except a bit dirtier.

Another phone call. You're told not to worry. The bathroom is almost finished.

But almost finished isn't the same as finished. In the same way as almost useable isn't the same as useable. When there's no water in a bathroom, it's not a bathroom; it's just a room with a bath in it. A 95 per cent bathroom is not a bathroom at all.

There's only so long someone can live without a bathroom. Only so long you can wash in a sink and poo in a bucket. Where *are* they? They're not pooing in a bucket. They've got bathrooms. That's one thing you can guarantee about builders. They've probably sorted out their bathrooms while leaving yours to rot. They won't be pooing in a bucket unless it's a thing that actually turns them on.

It doesn't turn you on. You get on the phone again. There seems to be have been some issues with something that is beyond your understanding. But there's good news: 'We will finish your bathroom on Monday.'

That's a cause for celebration at least. You'll be able to have a poo in your own home on Monday night, instead of trying to get rid of your excrement at work like you have been.

Except they don't turn up on Monday morning. Or Tuesday.

Now you are *cross*. You call. You tell them you are cross. Somehow they are more cross than you about it all. This confusing situation means you get less cross and sort of believe the flimsy reasons they give you for not turning up. You say you really need it sorted.

'We'll finish your bathroom on Monday,' they promise.

And this time a man turns up. One man. Then he leaves after fifteen minutes of fiddling with a pipe and talking on the phone in, possibly, Lithuanian. He never returns.

You call again. You get many apologies. You say you're not interested in that. You just want a bathroom. Otherwise you'll get someone else to do it.

They agree. You've had a bad time. They'll sort it out.

What can you do? The bathroom is almost finished. So tantalisingly close to being finished. It's almost a bathroom. And you've basically paid them anyway. They know your threat to get someone else in is an empty one.

And so you squat there, on a Sunday, pooing in a bucket. Safe in the knowledge that they will be coming to finish your bathroom on Monday.

This time you are sure of it . . .

Pretty sure . . .

LIE # **50**

" *I'll just do the washing-up*
and then I can start
my dissertation. **"**

It's not easy being a student. You don't have any money,
you tend to share a terrible flat with other dirty students
and you know that at the end of your course you face a
mountain of debt and a valley of job prospects. But on
the bright side you can laze about in bed all day eating
loads of crisps and watching daytime television. At least
that what's they say on Cliché Street and who am I to
argue?

But for every *Homes Under the Hammer* there's a
boring essay to write, and in your final year, the dreaded dissertation. Long after university has finished the
word 'dissertation' can strike fear into the heart of an
ex-student. Grown men have been known to wake in
the middle of the night screaming the word at the top
of their lungs. Grown women weep at bus stops convinced they've still not handed it in. If you want to ruin
the afternoon of a group of thirty-somethings sat in the
park, simply wander over and ask to see their disser-
tations. Before you know it they'll be crying into their

houmous and making a dash for the local library.*

The prospect of writing a dissertation is a daunting one and that's why so many people tell themselves the washing-up lie. It's the very last stop on the road of procrastination, and one final opportunity to avoid putting pen to paper or fingers to keys. Picture the scene. You're a twenty-something student pacing around a freezing cold flat in an old woolly jumper. You've got some books from the library and you've agreed with your tutor the topic of your dissertation. If you're a Philosophy student you might have ended up with something as dull as 'Exiting the Cave: Plato's Relevance to Contemporary Views of Body Image'. If you're an English student you might have found yourself lumbered with: 'Patriarchy and Gender Stereotyping in *The Chronicles of Narnia*'; and if you are a Sports Science student you're probably tackling 'Steve Bruce and the Horoscopes of the Hull City First Team'. Anyway, you've got several thousand words to write and an ever-looming deadline. So you smoke another roll-up.

Roll-up smoked, you plug in your laptop and put your books into a neat pile on the table beside you. Big ones at the bottom, small ones on top. No hang on, big ones to the left, small ones to the right. You quickly check Twitter

* Libraries were public buildings where people used to be able to go to borrow books for free. Nowadays they are mostly trainer shops or burger bars, and thank God for that. I mean, books are dull. Be honest, if this book was a trainer or a burger you would be much happier holding it than you are right now. Thank God they got rid of the libraries.

in case somebody's said anything about Plato, and make a cup of tea. Tea drunk, you check to see if the postman has been and then empty the bin. This hasn't been done for some time and it smells of death and gravy. You rearrange your books and check Facebook just in case somebody has posted a picture of Plato. They haven't but you notice that Gemma is having fun in Berlin. When did she write her dissertation? Maybe she hasn't. More fool her; if only she could see you now getting on with yours she wouldn't be kissing that man near the Brandenburg Gate. You open up a blank document and type the name of your dissertation along the top. You like it. It sounds very clever. *You* sound very clever. What will your parents think when they read it? You give your mum a call at work but Helen says she's gone to lunch with Pat. Lunch? Is that the time?

You go to the fridge and root around inside. There's something a bit brown in the salad drawer and an egg. This won't do, an academic marches on his stomach. You go to the Spar and buy some instant noodles. You walk the long way back just in case anyone's dropped a dissertation on Plato, and eat the noodles. They taste like the greatest thing you have ever eaten and you simply can't believe it when they've gone. You nip to the loo, then smoke a post-noodle roll-up, all the time wondering how Camus or J. K. Rowling got started. I bet they just got on with it you think. I bet they just ate their lunch and started typing.

164

Inspired, you return to your laptop and put your fingers on the home keys. And that's when you spot your dirty plate, and all the other dirty plates piled on the draining board. How are you meant to write in these conditions? This is no home for an intellectual. What is it they say about a tidy desk and a tidy mind? Well it must apply to draining boards as well. So you tell yourself the fiftieth lie of the day: 'I'll just do the washing-up and then I can start my dissertation.'

It takes considerably longer than you were expecting, but if you are going to do it you may as well do it properly, and there's no point in putting clean plates back in a dirty cupboard so you may as well give that a spruce with a damp rag while you're at it. And now it's 5 p.m. and that's much too late to start writing and anyway, it's got a bit chilly so you might as well have a bath.

If you're lucky, this entire process might repeat itself for a couple more days at most, then something imperceptible happens that forces you to get on with it. On some deeper level you realise you just have to get this thing over with, and start typing. Much like that bloke in *127 Hours* just had to get on with chopping his arm off. But the unlucky ones, well, they can be trapped in university for years. You sometimes see them stalking the corridors at night, or snuffling about in the darker corners of the library, fifty years of age, unshaven, looking for a book that isn't there. If you ever see one of these sorry cases, please treat them kindly. Take them home, sit them at their laptop and tell them it's going to be all right. They just need to get on with the writing, you are going to do the washing-up.

LIE # 51

Interests: travel, cinema
and socialising

One's curriculum vitae has always been seen as a place for, if not outright barefaced lying, then at least a place for some creativity when it comes to your definition of fact. How else do you think anyone gets a job? Or how I got this job?

'Everyone's doing it,' goes the thought, 'so I need to do it too, otherwise I'll miss out.' What does it matter if you exaggerate a little? Once you've got the job everyone will see how good you are.

And it's not like anyone checks CVs anyway. Has anyone ever actually been asked to bring in their GCSE certificates?

It seems like there is something in this reasoning – a recent survey has revealed that 12 per cent of employers admit that they spend less than thirty seconds looking at a CV. So why not let your imagination run wild on it? Maybe you did go to Oxford instead of Keele. Maybe you were made a senior manager at 24. Maybe you were the first drama student to visit the International Space Station.

However, there is a danger in this approach, because the same survey revealed that 71 per cent of employers have spotted a lie in someone's CV and have discarded the candidate as a result.

Outright lies are harder to get away with these days because of the internet, but a little 'artistic licence' is tricky to spot on the page. According to the survey, the most 'embellished' elements of a CV tend to be a candidate's skill set and responsibilities in a previous job, followed by some hocus-pocus with dates of employment, job titles and academic qualifications.

But perhaps the real sophistry on CVs isn't in the bare facts of employment and qualifications – it's the little section you are encouraged to write called 'Interests'. It's in this box, particularly in your early years climbing the greasy pole, that a certain 'editorialising' comes into play. Mainly because there's not much to write about in the space for 'Work History', but also because it's the one area that no one can check. If you say you're interested in bull fighting, who are they to doubt you? You may never have done anything that shows your interest in it, but no one can prove otherwise. Until they can look into your head. Which they're working on.

One 'interest' often remarked on is 'travel'. This makes the interviewer believe the candidate is daring, romantic, a risk-taker, broad in their horizons, willing to forsake creature comforts in exchange for the wisdom that can only be learned through a visit to the backwaters of Nepal. Although what the applicant really means is, they've been on holiday. Two weeks in Corfu with their mum and dad.

Another oft-listed 'interest' is 'cinema'. Just that – cinema. But the word 'cinema' leads employers to believe that a candidate spends all their time talking about Eric Rohmer and Jean Luc-Godard out the back of the BFI, when actually they've just illegally downloaded all the *Hangover* films. What they mean is: I like watching movies. *Like everyone does.*

And finally there's 'socialising'. There in black and white, this person likes socialising. Or to put it another way, they are not so withdrawn that they lock themselves in an attic room bottling their urine in anticipation of the apocalypse, and have at times been known to go to the pub with their mates.

Travel, cinema and socialising? Francis, move this one to the top of the pile and get them in for interview!

Have any of you ever lied about your interests on a CV?

Lee:

Oh yes, reading and swimming. I always put reading and swimming.

David:

Such incompatible hobbies.

And if an interviewer asked you what you liked to read?

Lee:

I'd say never mind that, let's talk about the swimming.

David:

It's always better to put swimming instead of drinking.

Lee, what was the last job you actually applied for with a CV?

Lee:

It was to work in the stockroom at WH Smith when I was a student. And the thing that genuinely motivated me to get on with this comedy malarkey was when the supervisor said to me: 'I cannot over-emphasise to you the importance of the organisation of the stockroom pencils.' And that was the moment when I thought: 'I'm going to get into showbiz, I can't do this any longer.'

Rob:

Did he mean by hardness of points?

Lee:

It was all sorts of things – the hardness, whether they had rubbers on the end – I literally had to go round the stockroom with a list and find what we were missing in the shop. So I might have to get four HBs with a rubber on the end, two 2Bs without rubbers, a 6H and an F.

Rob:

So they *had* to be perfectly organised. You know what? The more I hear about these pencils, the more I'm on that guy's side.

David, have you ever lied on a CV?

David:

I once put 'fluent French' when I was trying to get work as an actor.

Lee:

Oh, in case you got a part?

David:

Yes, in case someone said, 'Actually, we need you to play Maigret in France.' What I *didn't* put, but what I was encouraged to put by my agent, was that I could ride a horse. I can't ride a horse, and I didn't want them to find that out after I'd been cast to gallop around and sweep damsels off their feet.

Rob:

Horse riding's a big one for actors isn't it? I can do all sorts of horse stuff.

David:

I've been on a horse twice. I've sat on one on one occasion, and on another occasion I sort of trundled along on one. So I've had one stationary horse experience, and one actual moving experience.

Rob:

The stationary one interests me. You got on the horse, you went 'OK' and you got off the horse.

David:

I think I was about five, and the people who lived across the road, their daughter liked horse riding, and they said, 'Would you like to sit on the horse?' and they put me on the horse, and I went, 'GET ME OFF THE HORSE!' I also went to a wildlife park, where you could be led along a track on an exhausted, defeated pony who looked like his stuffing had come out.

Lee:

I lied about horse manure once. When I worked at the stables with Red Rum [true – see *Would I Lie To You?* series one] I used to go round door to door selling manure for fifty pence a bag. I would

172

knock and say: 'Do you want to buy some manure? It's Red Rum's.'

Rob:

Was it Red Rum's?

Lee:

It was lots of horses'. Red Rum couldn't produce the amount I was selling.

David:

I daresay it wasn't sorted horse by horse. It's like the ashes at a crematorium. They tell you it's your granny, but really it's just a spoonful of everyone.

LIE # 52

"I was going to say that!"

Take a seat alongside any pub quiz team and this is what you'll find. One very clever person with an impressive all-round general knowledge. This is usually a woman. One fairly clever person with a solid all-round general knowledge. This is usually a man. (This man is often envious of the woman's superior knowledge and so takes control of the pen and the answer sheets in order to establish dominance around the table.) Someone who knows everything about sport but nothing else. Someone who is drunk. Someone who has to leave early but is very good at the picture quiz (YES! That *is* Lionel Richie!). And a complete idiot who gets everything wrong yet insists on shouting 'I was going to say that!' when the answers are read out.

You know and I know that they were *never* going to say that or else they would have said it, but again and again they protest like a . . . boring idiot at a pub quiz.

Question 1: the answer was November 1963.
    I was going to say that!

Question 2: we were looking for Xenon.
    I was going to say that!

Question 3: he was dancing on the . . . *ceiling*.
    I was going to say that!

Never is this characteristic more irritating than when gathered around the pub quiz machine. You know the drill, the big-screen football match has finished and a giant Jamie Carragher is failing to hold the interest. So you wander over to the quiz machine and drop a pound coin into its metal face. You're doing quite well when you sense the presence of the 'quiziot' behind you. With every new question he sucks his teeth to indicate it's trickiness, then applauds and pats you on the back when you get it right. Suddenly, you're faced with a question outside of your comfort zone, and out of desperation you see if he can help.

'Was *The Godfather* released in 1972 or 1973?' you ask.

'Ooh, good question,' he says, dropping his peanuts. 'I think it was seventy-three, but it might be seventy-two.'

Time is running out.

'Was that the one with John Travolta?' he asks.

'Brando,' you say.

'That's it. Love that film. It was seventy-three. I'm certain it was seventy-three.'

You really don't know, and as the time is almost out you hit the button for seventy-three.

It's wrong. Game over. You've lost.

'I knew it was seventy-two,' he says. 'I was going to say that.'

For a brief moment you consider murder, but then you notice that the giant Jamie Carragher has been replaced by an episode of *A League of Their Own*, so you return to your table and watch John Bishop hit an onion with a tennis racket.

Meanwhile, someone else feeds some silver into the machine and the irritant takes his familiar position at the rear. In an act of civic duty you call over a warning to the quizzer: 'Don't ask him anything,' you bellow, 'he hasn't got a clue what he's talking about.' And for perhaps the only time in his life the berk doesn't reply with, 'I was going to say that.'

LIE # 53

"*I'm definitely not stalking you!*"

You met briefly at the gym. She was having a coffee, you a carrot juice vanilla zest infusion recovery shake bottle. You chatted innocently about nothing. She seemed nice enough, though you didn't rate her trainers and were soon on your way.

The next day you receive a tweet. 'Hope you don't think I'm stalking you! Was great to meet you yesterday! See you again at the gym!' You are flattered and surprised. She had almost nothing to go on: you mentioned that you enjoy cage fighting, are a man and are studying for a PhD in female nudity and the plays of Gerald Snott. You consult Google and find her on LinkedIn, before quickly logging off. Can she tell you've looked at her profile? You can't remember, so you finish up your whey tuna protein flaxseed oil chocolate shake with low fat sugar, and hit the hay.

Two days later you receive a friend request on Facebook. You are beginning to feel stalked but remain flattered. Curious, you look at her pictures: there are many images of her holding alcohol of varying shades up towards the camera. She is reasonable looking and appears to be single but you feel hunted so log off. Then you log back on and look at her photographs again. Can she tell you've looked at her photos? You can't remember so you finish your soy almond oatmeal mixed berry creatine recovery shake with *frankincense*, and turn in.

Another day passes. You forget all about your stalker and press on with your PhD, focusing in particular on the play 'Kiss Me or Die or Maybe Neither' during which the character Susan Spoot dramatically removes a bra made out of paper. You write three paragraphs about the scene, do 119 press-ups then feel tired. You lie down and check your email.

> 'I hope you don't think I'm stalking you but I found your address on your university page so I thought I'd drop you a line! Was lovely to meet you the other day! It's not often you feel such a connection with someone! You obviously felt the same because you've been looking at my LinkedIn profile and Facebook pictures! Anyway I'm definitely not stalking you just wanted to say hi!! xxx'

You suddenly realise that, sat on the sofa in your own flat, you feel scared. You rise and drop the blinds, then open them an inch. Is that her lurking by the postbox? Of course not, that's Animal Rachel from downstairs. You're seeing things.

You take a bath. While lying there in your own dirt you check your phone. Your stalker has 'favourited' seventeen of your tweets, even the boring one about being 'tired of the democratic process'. You turn off your phone, climb out of the bath, cry a bit and dry yourself. Then you check there isn't a bunny in a pot on the hob, even though you don't own a bunny, or a hob.

You lie back down on the sofa and search your TV hard drive for something reassuring. You settle on *Look East*. No sooner have you started watching than the doorbell rings. You lie there frozen. It goes again. Terrified, you bundle all the remote controls together and hug them. After two minutes you find the courage to peer once more through the blinds. As you do, you see the gasman leaving.

There's only one cure for this anxiety: exercise. Oh look, in seventeen minutes there's a Bodypump Boxercise Kettlebell Kickboxing™ session at the gym. But hold on. The gym? You can't go to the gym! She might be waiting!

You call them up and cancel your membership. Next you delete your Facebook and Twitter accounts, and close down your email account. Finally, you ring the estate agents to tell them you need to move out as soon as possible. A woman answers.

'Paul? Is that you? It's me! Sue! From the gym!'

LIE # 54

"I've got a hospital appointment."

So, you need to leave work for a bit of the day. A middle bit of the day. And you can't tell ANYONE at work.

Why do you actually need to leave? And why can't you tell ANYONE?

Because you have a job interview. For a job much better than the one you have right now. And you want that to remain a secret.

You could take the whole day off. But that seems a bit of a waste of a holiday day. Especially if you don't get the job. It will have been a total waste of a day off, a day off you could take later in the year to see the new Star Wars film at its first showing.

You could try one of the usual office lies, like waiting for a delivery or going to the doctor's. But they're sort of morning things, they won't explain you leaving the office and not coming back again. And they especially won't explain why you had to cancel the meetings you'd arranged for the day.

So you have to go straight to the ace of spades when it comes to leaving work: 'I have to go now, I've got a hospital appointment.'

This trumps even 'doctor's appointment' because it suggests that what you have, even though there is no outside evidence of any illness, is very, very serious indeed. A doctor's appointment, you might just have a cold. You'll have to pretend to sneeze for a bit for that to add up. A hospital could mean you are about to die. So no one is going to say, 'Will you be back by three for the meeting?'

And a hospital appointment also means that it's perfectly understandable that you have totally rearranged and cancelled the day's work. You have to take a hospital appointment when it comes, you can't pick and choose.

On playing the hospital card though, most people will normally just go, 'Oh, OK', and be too worried and embarrassed to ask what it is. You might feel the need to follow up with a brief explanation of what it is – back pain or something non-contagious like that. But don't. The more you say undermines the power of the lie. The most someone will say is, 'Everything OK?' To which you just nod.

You don't want to scare people; you don't want them to think you actually have something, you know, hospitally. But if people look suspicious you can always add the words 'just some tests' to shut them up, and you can merrily go off to your job interview.

The next day your colleagues will have forgotten about the hospital appointment. They won't mention it ever again. Because they know that the words 'hospital appointment' really mean 'job interview'. They know this because they've all used the very same excuse. They also know that if you turn up for work the next week, you didn't get the job, and if you're still at work the week after that, you don't have a deadly disease.

Exercises

1. Work out a better way of getting out of work than a hospital appointment. (You can't, there isn't one.)

2. You are a hospital doctor who has a job interview. What do you tell your boss?

55

" *I really need this new phone.* "

Because the thing is, my old phone, my old phone is like, what? Coming up for a year old? Almost. And this new phone is going to blow it out of the water. It's going to basically make my phone go from being a phone to being a useless piece of prehistoric rubbish.

What's so good about this new phone? What's so good about it? Why do I need it so much? Let me tell you.

For a start, it's new. It's a new model. It's the latest model. The newest. There's no newer model of phone than this. Until a new one comes out. My old phone, it used to be the newest, but now it's really like, amongst the oldest.

I really need this new phone.

Another thing about it is that it's a bit thinner. How much? A bit. A little bit. Like a millimetre or something. But that's crucial. That's what makes it so good. Although when it's in a case you won't really notice.

And its screen is a bit bigger. A little bit bigger. So things will be bigger on the screen. A little bit.

And it's faster. I think it's faster. It actually is really fast.

It's like 2 per cent faster than my current phone. Although it depends how fast the actual connection is.

Sure, it can do all the things my current phone can do. Of course it can. It can make calls and send messages and run email and look at the web and use apps and stuff. So that's great. I mean, it doesn't do anything *new*, but it's a phone, why would it?

Yes, it looks sort of the same, but a little bit different so none of my current chargers will work with it. But here's another reason I really need this new phone. They've done this really cool thing where it comes in a colour you couldn't get it in before. It's a sort of silver-gold-teak kind of colour. So people will know it's a new phone, not an old phone. Although I guess once I've put it in a cover you won't see what colour it is.

And another thing. My old phone, it's well, it's not not-working yet but it might start not-working soon. So I should probably pre-empt that and get this new phone.

Yes, I could spend the money on something else. Like a deposit for a house. Or a holiday. Or give it to charity. But you're forgetting the key thing here.

I really need this new phone.

Exercise

1. Try not buying the latest phone. For a bit.

56

> **❝** I love both my children equally
> and don't have a favourite. **❞**

You love your children more than you love yourself, and
for you that's a big deal. How could nature create such
perfection? Your heart is split equally between them.

Is it though? Of course not!

You say you love them equally. You may even pretend
to yourself that you do. But you don't. You don't even
like your own hands the same, how could you love two
entirely different human entities identically?

'Yes, but I love them in different ways!' you respond
defensively. No one believes you.

If only George could be more like Bridget. Bridget is
so funny. And clever. With George, it's different. It's not
as if you're not fond of him. On his day he's eminent-
ly likeable. Plus he's showing a great aptitude for maths.
But, well, there's something about him that's, what's the
word . . . *unappealing*. That's it: he's unappealing.

Is it the neediness? He *is* quite needy. And weird.
Needy and weird. It's not the ideal combination. Also
what's with that smell? No one else in the family smells
like that. It's like he's not even yours.

Of course, you experience constant guilt about these feelings and attempt to mask them by endlessly bigging him up. 'He's amazing at fractions!' you say. 'And he can do a passable impression of darts champion Eric Bristow!' But it's a giveaway. Your friends can tell you're overcompensating, talking up his modest achievements, pretending to care. People can smell your ambiguity.

Perhaps you've made him like this. You took against him from the off and he sensed it. Oh my God, it's all down to you. Your son's weird because you didn't like his smell. But is that really your fault? Of course not. It's chemical! It's science! Some smells we are designed to get along with, others not. There was nothing you could do about that. You can't fight nature.

He's probably a late bloomer. That's what it is. He'll grow into himself, flourish and then you'll warm to him a little rather than feeling constantly annoyed by him and his hapless ways. Some kids just take that little bit longer to find their feet. Because they're weird.

It's a shame he isn't sporty though. I mean, you're sporty and so is your partner and so is Bridget. Bridget is *so* sporty! She loves all sports, her favourites being running and swimming and golf and hockey and rounders and karate and real tennis. George doesn't even *like* sport. How can this be? Sometimes you wonder whether there was a mix-up at the hospital. Also, why doesn't he smile more? If only he smiled more people would love him. Maybe *you'd* even love him. Jeez, he is *so annoying*.

The worst thing about all this is that you fear it reflects badly on you, that you are somehow deficient as a parent. Typical George, making you feel bad about yourself. No wonder you struggle to love him. Not that George is his real name. For the purposes of this book you decided to change it to protect his identity. You can't say what from, although it rhymes with 'Bistopher'.

Lies to watch out for from . . . **Estate Agents**

LIE # 57

Estate agents, with their cheap suits and expensive houses have made a profession out of telling lies. They lie when you're buying and they lie when you sell. They lie face to face and they lie on the phone. They lie in emails and they lie in texts. They lie in the morning and they lie at night. They lie in the shower and they lie in the bath. They lie at breakfast and they lie at lunch. They lie to their colleagues and they lie to their friends. They lie to their clients and they lie to themselves. Their breath may be minty, their aftershave cheap, still all you can smell are the lies.

When estate agents aren't lying they like to offend us in other ways. They put-put around town in stupid cars listening to awful radio stations. They sing along to advertising jingles with the windows rolled down. They wear fake tan and hair gel. They have irritating ringtones and ugly pointed shoes. They chew gum and high-five each other. They drop litter and talk about targets. They pick their noses on the phone. They loiter on driveways holding A4 leather wallets. They chew the ends of their pens. They exist.

Here is a handy guide to cutting through the nonsense of estate agent jargon. Ignore it at your peril.

Compact/bijou If this were a prison cell, it would be deemed to small for occupancy.

Sleepy hamlet Swingers welcome!

Up-and-coming area No murders since Tuesday.

A stone's throw from At least five stops on the bus.

A project Most of the walls are missing and one of the rooms was previously used for dog fighting.

Quirky decor The most disgusting wallpaper you have ever seen in your life.

Sought-after street The most overpriced street in the area, near a good school.

Competitively priced for quick sale Landlord has gambling debts.

Investment opportunity You would never in a million years want to live in it yourself.

Decorated to a high standard They've run a Hoover round.

City views You can see the tip of The Shard behind a multi-storey car park.

Architect-designed Feels like a mortuary with a TV in the ceiling.

Are there any particular group of people you associate with telling lies?

Lee:

Family! They're not always there for you. They say they love you, and then they just change their feelings about you when you end up doing a short time in borstal. And can you please emphasise the *short*.

LIE # 58

" *I'm not too old to be in here.* "

I'm not too be old to be in here. Yes, it's a bar mainly filled with younger people. Much, much younger people. But I still fit in. I mean nobody thinks it's weird that I'm in here. Even though everyone else here is younger. Much younger. I mean I am old, older, but I'm not too old to be in here.

Actually, look, over there. He's older than me. Much older. Well, at least as old. About the same age probably, maybe a bit younger. But he dresses much older. Those trousers are for a man much older than him. My trousers are really young. They're young trousers. Young people's trousers. From a young people's trouser shop. Heart-stoppingly expensive young people's trousers. How young people afford them, I don't know, I thought they had no money and were all living in Zone 6 near the Overground. My legs look like those of a twenty-five-year-old. And my shirt is young too. Youngish. Just in an oldish size.

And that woman he's with. She must be almost my age – give or take ten years. Mainly take. Or give. Which ever one means younger. But she's in my age bracket. In opinion polls, she'd be bracketed with me. 18–24, 25–34, 35–44, etc. She's in my general bracket. Or the one immediately below.

I mean, it doesn't matter how old you are, it's how old you feel. Your sensibility. Your loves, your life. And I feel young. I don't feel too old to be in here. And you can tell that from the way I hold myself. From the way I stand. Be good to get a seat though.

Why do I come here? Do I like the music? No, I can't really hear myself think 'I'm not too old to be in here'. But I like the ambience. The lighting. The mise-en-scene. Although the near semi-darkness does make it difficult to finish off the *Guardian* quiz. Especially without the bifocals on. I guess I'll never know what connects Gin Rummy, Tolstoy, witch hazel and the Forth Road Bridge now. Not in this light.

I don't look too old to be in here: my beard makes me look young. Because young men have beards. So I look young. Although, conversely, a beard also makes you look older. If I shave it off, will I look younger or older? A bit of a catch-22 situation. Should ask Mandy at work. She's nice. Friendly. Maybe I should see what's she's been doing on Facebook. Need to ask her who that boy is in her holiday photos.

How do they afford all these drinks? These young people? Cocktails at £10.90? I'll stick to Amstel. Can't go wrong with Amstel. And most of the time they're on their phones. Expensive place to come to look at Twitter and check out the times of the Overground trains.

She's pretty. Is she too young for me? Well she's younger than me. Obviously. Is that a bad thing? Well as long as she's not *that* young, that would be a bad thing. What's that French rule? The ideal pairing is a woman whose age is half the man's age plus seven years. So, I could be with a . . . hang on . . . quite hard after four Amstels . . . well, someone younger. In France. I don't know if it's a rule or a law in France. Maybe it is a law and that's why they all get mistresses. They do lead a good life. Hedonistic. Might go there for a mini-break in the Alfa.

She looks clever. I mean pretty, yes. But I'm beyond all that. She does look like she's clever. Maybe she's a cultural analyst. Or a curator. Or a social media expert. Or French. Yes, I think she might be French. I think she might be. She's drinking wine. House white. I'm old enough now to appreciate a woman for her brain, rather than her looks. As long as she has nice legs. That's a deal breaker. But luckily these days a lot of brainy women do have nice legs. Like Lauren Laverne, Emily Maitlis and Emma Willis.

She looks kind of cool. Cool enough for me to talk to. Intelligent. If I was ten years younger . . . or more. If only I'd been able to finish that *Guardian* quiz we could talk about that. I bet she finished it. And made one of Ottelenghi's Broccoli Fritters with Harissa.

Is she looking at me? Wish it wasn't quite so dark. Wish I could put on the bifocals. But might make me seem old.

Catch-22. Maybe she *is* looking at me? She must like my trousers. Oh, yeah, these trousers were worth every penny. She likes my trousers.

She's waving – that's – oh, she's waving at a friend behind me. A boy. Her boyfriend? Maybe. She's kissing him. But she's young. These young flings never last long. No real depth. I have depth to offer. And an ex-local-authority flat in Primrose Hill, which is worth a bomb these days. Even though it's near the bins.

No one's bothered by the fact I'm a bit older. They don't care. They don't judge people by how old they are. It's all about what phone you've got these days. I've got an Apple iPhone 6 Plus. The big one. It fits in my pocket. Almost. Sticks out a bit and squashes into my balls on the train, but it looks good. Expensive. Good to read in a dark bar. I'll just see how Fulham got on in the late kick-off.

Yes, I'm not too old to be in here. Everyone is totally oblivious to me. All happily, totally obvious to me, just all talking young people's things and checking their phones, totally ignoring me while I stand in the dark with my Amstel. I totally fit in with them. I'm not too old to be in here, at all.

LIE # **59**

"I didn't get the message."

Since the dawn of time people have pretended not to receive important messages. Here's a brief chronological history:

Sorry, but I can't understand you because language hasn't been invented yet.

Sorry, didn't get your cave painting.

Sorry, didn't get your smoke signal.

What messenger boy?

Your carrier pigeon must have been poisoned by the Holy Roman Empire.

Letter? Sorry, I don't have a letterbox.

Never got your Morse code.

My fax machine is out of paper.

My email's been playing up.

Can't get texts here in Swindon.

Our WhatsApps must be different versions.

Sorry, your invitation never uploaded into my brainchip.

People like to wriggle out of stuff because it means they can do other stuff instead. The nature of the wriggle may have changed, but the desire to do so remains the same.

Picture the scene: it's a glorious Saturday afternoon in Ashby-de-la-Zouch and a select group of you is about to head out for an evening of fun, frolics and controlled drinking. Suddenly, you receive a text from Derek the Knob.

'It's me lol! What you doing tonight! I'm around!'

Derek's a knob (you can tell by his nickname) but he hangs around and, like a piano, is hard to shift. For once he's gone quiet and you've arranged to go out without him. If he comes along it will ruin the evening – and quite possibly the year – so you don't reply.

The next day he calls.

'Did you get my message?' he asks.

'What message?' you lie.

'The one that according to my phone you received.'

Herein lies a problem. Today people can often see whether a message is 'received', 'sent' and so on. You stand firm.

'Sorry, Derek, didn't get a message.'

'That's weird, it said the message had been received and read. Can I come round to your house and verify this information?'

'You're breaking up,' you say and hang up.

He calls back.

'You said I was breaking up.'

'That's right.'

'I've never broken up before. I'm sat at home with a perfect signal. The signal is always great at your house too.'

'I'm in Outer Mongolia,' you tell him.

'Really?'

'Yes.'

'Then how come it didn't do the foreign ringtone?' he asks.

'Got to go, about to be eaten by a Mongolian shark,' you say, hanging up again, and hurling your phone into a bucket of water.

The challenge with 'didn't get the message' is that your lie may be researchable to the point of you being labelled a fibber. In such instances it is best to front it out, have the other party assassinated, or something in between.

The truth (not a word you'll hear often within these pages) is that you should probably tell Derek the Knob you don't enjoy spending time with him. Although painful for both of you (especially, if you're honest, Derek) ultimately this will help Derek find new friends while freeing you up to spend more time on the loose in Ashby-de-la-Zouch. And why not, it's such a great place. No, I'm deadly serious. Probably going there again next week. Yes, of course, you can come along. What day? Not sure yet. What was that? You what? Sorry, you're breaking up . . .

60

" *I didn't have that much to drink.* **"**

If I'd had a lot to drink last night I'd understand why I feel so bad this morning. But the thing is, I didn't. So why have I got this terrible hangover? I just don't get why I've got it so bad, I think that I might be ill with something, because actually, I didn't have that much to drink.

I mean I had *something* to drink. I had something. It would be weird to feel like this after nothing to drink. But no more than normal. I mean maybe a bit more than normal. But what's normal? Maybe my normal is someone else's less than average? Or average. Or more than average. I don't know. I don't keep a record of how much everyone's drinking, I'm not some kind of alcohol Nazi.

I mean I did probably start drinking early. Because it was whatshername's birthday and we had Prosecco and cake in the office. It was warm – the Prosecco, not the cake – so I couldn't really drink more than three plastic cups of it. And also because there was none left after a bit. But I did line my stomach with two slices of cake. And I didn't feel the slightest bit drunk afterwards. I wrote three more emails after that, and one was an important one. It was only internal, but it was pretty important.

So, I really didn't have that much to drink. I'm totally baffled as to why I feel so ropey. Yes, I did go to the pub with the guys from the fifth floor but it was only a normal Tuesday night sort of thing. I didn't keep count of the drinks – who does? – but only must have had, what? A couple of glasses of wine. And a gin and tonic. And a vodka tonic. And maybe – were there some shots? Right at the end? But that doesn't explain why I've just been sick in the drawer of my bedside cabinet. Because I didn't have that much to drink.

I mean, yes, I did have more than my recommended daily units of alcohol. But then everyone does. No one sticks to that. But did I have enough to warrant feeling this bad? No. I have to say, I don't think so. And actually, when I think about it, I had almost all of my five a day yesterday (if crisps count, which no one can actually tell me) so that should actually be making me feel better.

And then a few of us went to the Wetherspoons for something to eat. Soak up the booze a bit (another reason I shouldn't feel as bad as I do – I did eat, which is unusual for me). There was an offer on. I had a burger and a pint. And then another pint. But not another burger. Who eats two burgers? If I'd done that, that would explain why I feel so bad.

And then I came home. And maybe I had a brandy watching Netflix on the laptop. Or a couple of brandies.

And the last of the Tia Maria. And one of those pre-mix Marks and Spencer's Mojitos in a can I found in the back of the fridge. And then I drank something someone brought back from Belize and fell asleep with my clothes on.

So it's just so weird, that I feel so, so wretched. I think I should maybe call the doctor's. Or my mum. Or whatever NHS Direct is called now. Or maybe I'll Google something relevant when I can think of what something relevant would be.

Because I'm really worried. I'm really concerned. I feel terrible. I feel like I'm dying. And I didn't have that much to drink.

LIE # 61

The Coffee Shop lie

You fancy a coffee. You always fancy coffee. Face it, you're an addict. Most addicts favour drugs or booze. Not you. You're addicted to a hot brown drink. You've even got one of those special metallic cups you carry around. Man, you've got problems.

You enter a coffee shop and wait your turn, surveying the cakes, scones, muffins and cookies. 'My word, they look good enough to eat,' you mutter quietly. 'These people really know how to put on a display.' But you deny yourself, because you're only here for the coffee. Nothing else matters in your life, not even Claire.

'A flat white mocca chocca latte dark blend with an extra shot and skimmed milk please,' you say, shaking. 'And a glass of tap water.'

'Anything else?'

'If I'd wanted anything else I would have asked for it. Just coffee. That's all I ever want. Give me coffee now.'

'£2.95 please. And your name?'

They ask for your name. They always ask for your name. You get it, it's so they can announce when your drug of choice is ready. But you have a deeply embarrassing name. So you lie.

'Judith,' you say. You give a woman's name, even though you are a man. You got confused because you had to give a false name. Never mind, at least it's not as embarrassing as your real name.

'Thanks, Judith, your drink will be ready in a couple of minutes.'

You move towards the serving area and remain there, playing with a couple of sugar sachets behind your back.

As lies go it's hardly a biggie, but it's still a lie. You've always lied about your name; never want to draw attention to yourself. That's not your bag or pigeon. In your position anyone would do the same. If anything, your endeavour is to be applauded (your coffee addiction less so).

Of course, you're not the only one. You know a woman called 'Marge' who calls herself 'Adrianna' at Starbucks.

'What's wrong with "Marge"?' you're always asking her. 'It's a nice name. And it's not *nearly* as bad as mine.'

'Ever since I was a little kid growing up in Oadby I wanted to be "Adrianna",' says Marge. 'This way I get to play out the fantasy.'

'Fair enough,' you tell Marge.

'Though you're right,' she continues, 'my name isn't a *tenth* as embarrassing as yours.'

'Thanks,' you reply.

Your coffee-shop name is yours to call. Got a long one?

Shorten it. An embarrassing one? Change it, especially if you're 'Myra' or 'Adolf'. Some switch their name to sound cool because they're standing next to a man or woman they would like to kiss on the mouth. Others give silly names simply to hear them said out loud, such as 'Willy' or 'Bloomscababu'.

But you have a special reason. Because you have the worst name in history.

'Judith!'

It dawns on you someone has been calling 'Judith' for the past minute. You didn't make the connection because that's not your real name. You collect your coffee and say thank you in a woman's voice. You have no idea why you do this and hurry out the door. Outside you bump into an old friend.

'Hey, Anus, how's it going?'

LIE # 62

" That looks really great on you. **"**

Clothes shop assistants *must lie*. It's their job. It's the main part of their job.

(Minor duties include looking at you like you don't belong in the shop, and following closely behind you refolding jumpers because you have had the temerity to unfold.)

But the main part of their job, the key part, is they *must lie*.

If they didn't lie, if they told the truth every time someone tried something on, they'd never sell anything. That's why you never hear these words uttered by a shop assistant:

'Yeah, that makes you look really fat.'
'That colour clashes violently with your skin tone.'
'It makes you the shape of a pile of vomit.'
'That style is not coming back in.'
'You look like a total wally in that.'
'I don't think you can really pull that look off.'
'That look is way too young for you.'
'LOL.'

'*That makes me feel physically ill. Please step out of it now.*'

'*It makes you look like Yoko Ono.*'

'*Let me take your picture. This will be a really funny GIF for a Buzzfeed list I'm compiling of 22 Reasons Old People Shouldn't Go Shopping.*'

'*No.*'

Instead, they have to say: 'That looks *really* great on you.'

Of course, you're ready for that. You know shop assistants *must lie*. But here's the bit you might not know: the shop assistants *know* you know. They *know*. That's what they're told at the staff meetings they have on Tuesday mornings.

They know 'that looks really great on you' is not going to cut any ice, so they say: 'That looks *really* great on you.'

The key thing is the stress on the '*really*'. Not 'really great' but '*really* great'.

Do they mean '*really*' as in 'very'? Are they saying this is more than just the average amount of 'really good' that they tell everyone else?

Or do they mean '*really*' as in 'actually'? As in: 'I lie to every other person in here about how things look good on them, but weirdly, this piece of man-made fabric stitched together by a ten-year-old in Burma does *actually* look good on you.'

(Sometimes they also try to introduce a sense of self-amazement about this, as if they hadn't expected it to look good on you and had in fact expected the complete opposite. They say the '*really*' with a sort of acted half-smile, as in, 'If I'm honest, I thought you were going to look like a complete idiot and I genuinely would have let you know that, but actually, you have surprised me, you've made me readdress my prejudices and preconceptions. Thank you.' This technique is dangerous in anyone below the rank of assistant manager. It demands precision and heft.)

You know shop assistants *must lie*, but the ambiguity of the meaning of '*really*' is momentarily baffling.

So, you buy it. And at home you realise:

You don't look *really* good.

You don't even look really good.

You look . . . all right.

At best, *all right.*

Do you chaps enjoy clothes shopping?

David:
Is that a comment on our ill-fitting garments?

Rob:
You do realise that you're dealing with three guys who don't do our own shopping any more. We send someone. I have a guy who's my height, my build—

Lee
Janette Krankie.

Rob:
Thank you, Lee. And he goes and tries things on for me. I basically send Anton du Beke to a shop, he stoops, and if it looks good on him, I'll have it.

David:
I've never discussed with a stranger who works in a shop what I look like in any clothes I've tried on. I might go into the cubicle and try something on, have a look, go, does that fit? How much of an idiot do I look? Then take it off, put my normal clothes on and leave. But I'm never going to discuss that with a stranger, I find it awkward enough with people I know.

Rob:
Well, I actually like shopping and I have a few shops I go to where I know the people and I consider them friends.

David:

I find that very odd.

Rob:

And I like clothes shopping with my wife as well. I like clothes shopping for her clothes, and I like trying them on at home when she's not there.

Lee:

I find *that* very odd.

LIE # 63

"It's not you, it's me.**"**

In the words of Neil Sedaka (ask your parents) breaking up is hard to do. That's why it really helps if one of you in the relationship has done something so bad it's impossible for the union to continue. Painful though it might be, it's quite easy to split up with somebody if they've been cheating on you. You can sit them down and say, 'Look—'(let's call her Debra) 'Look, Debra, I do love you, at least I *did* love you, but I'm finding it really hard to deal with the fact that you slept with all those guys from the circus last weekend. I know I'd maybe not been around that much lately, what with me being cooped up in the office all hours writing the *Would I Lie To You?* book, but I thought you had more respect for me than to go to the circus and sleep with ALL the guys who work there in one evening. And it really upset me to find out via Facebook. I can't believe you posted pictures of the whole thing. You and the circus guys looked like you were having so much fun, and seeing how fit and flexible they were has done absolutely nothing for my own body image. And why blog about it? How is that supposed to help? Even the title of your blog post hurt me: "How one incredible night with twelve fit strangers from the circus made me feel like a woman for the first time in five years." I feel betrayed by you, Debra, and I have decided to end our relationship.'

You see, in this instance, the break-up is a straightforward one. The fictional author of the *Would I Lie To You?* book has been viciously wronged by his fictional girlfriend of five years, and she can have no complaints that he has decided to end their relationship. What would be nice is if she was a little more understanding when the fictional author turned up at her new flat in the middle of the night and begged her to come back. If a fictional author can find it in his bruised and battered heart to forgive his ex-girlfriend for having a lust marathon with twelve of the fittest guys ever to work the attractions of a travelling circus, then the least the fictional girlfriend can do is entertain the idea of reconciliation. But such is the complexity of fictional relationships.

Not all couples, however, break up because of circus swinging, or indeed any kind of infidelity. Sometimes relationships just shrivel to nothing and die. Very often this death is felt more keenly by one person than the other, and that's when the 'It's not you, it's me' lie is introduced to ease the passage of separation.

'It's not you, it's me' means I don't love you any more. There are things that you do that irritate me, and there are things that I wish you would do that you don't do.

But rather than blame you for your imperfections as I see them, I will pretend that you are perfect and that the problem resides with me. It is my fault that I don't appreciate your annoying laugh and it's my fault that you crack your knuckles when you watch *A Question of Sport* (which you have series-linked). It's my fault that you say things like 'hashtag sad face' and it's my fault that you don't ever want to go out any more. It's my fault that your friends are, without exception, hateful people; and it's my fault that you wear stupid clothes and read stupid books. It's my fault that you can't tell a joke without ruining the punch line and it's my fault that you make really boring observations about things I'm not interested in. It's my fault that you are learning the didgeridoo and it's my fault that you like Mumford and Sons. It's my fault that you drink your coffee from a Purple Ronnie mug and it's my fault that you say that you can juggle on your CV. But most of all, it's my fault that every time I hear your key in the lock my heart fills with sickness and regret and I think about ways to escape this suffocating relationship that is sucking all the joy from my fleeting appearance on this magnificent, but ultimately insignificant, planet.

And this is where the next lie in this break-up sequence is always introduced

'Whatever happens [Debra], I want us to be friends.'

LIE # 64

66 I'm not addicted to social media. 99

'That was funny,' you say.
  'What was?'
  'That thing you said. About gnomes. Say it again.'
  'Why?'
  'I want to tweet it.'

Everything that happens to you, everything you see or hear, finds its way onto social media. You're addicted.

'I'm not addicted!' you say.
  'You're tweeting as you say that.'
  'I'm simply cataloguing my life for future generations,' you reply.

You post a funny link on Facebook. Within half an hour twenty-three people have seen it. 'Why have none of them liked it?' you ask. 'I need someone to validate my existence.' You refresh the page every thirty seconds. At last a like comes through from a person you haven't seen since 1983.

'Thanks for the like, Duncan!' you write, hoping he'll reply. If he does that will be one like and two comments, thereby making your timeline look busy and filling the emptiness inside. Duncan doesn't reply but look, another like, this time from someone you've never met. This is turning out to be a great day.

You don't go anywhere without your phone. One day last July you left it at home. It was only when you saw a dead pigeon with a passing resemblance to Princess Anne that you realised your mistake. You've not made such an error since (the pigeon post garnered twenty-six likes and nineteen comments).

You won't acknowledge you have a problem, mainly because you haven't looked up or had a normal conversation since 2009. No one's seen the underside of your chin since the London Olympics. Your friends expressed concern when you Instagrammed a selfie with your dead grandmother in the background but you laughed it off, then blogged about it.

Once upon a time you enjoyed conversation, finger puppetry and other pastimes. You used to criticise people who used emoticons. Not any more. You are lost to the virtual world.

'You'd tweet as much as me if you had 2,949 followers,' you say. 'I have a responsibility to give my audience regular updates. Did you know my tweet about Donald Trump's hair got twenty-seven retweets? What are you doing with *your* life?'

Your friends are considering a twintervention. They want you back. If that means hurling your phone into the Thames and holding you down as you go cold turkey, so be it. They realise there are risks (you might go crazy then document your madness on Tumblr) but they're in for the long haul.

You reach 3,000 followers on Twitter and decide to hold a virtual party.

'Thanks for coming!' you tweet. 'Make yourselves at home, pass round the Twit-glets and lets get this party started! #myparty #bringabottle.'

'Thanks for inviting me,' says @simonthepieman13. 'By the way you're a MASSIVE LOSER. Go out and get some proper friends LOSER.'

You are inconsolable, which means constantly posting how wounded you feel all over social media. Other people who are equally lost come to your aid and administer virtual hugs. After three days you are feeling more robust.

'The person who hurt my feelings needs to get a life!' you write on Twitter and Facebook and Bebo and Google+ simultaneously, before refreshing the pages for comments.

LIE # 65

" Exciting new concept coming soon. "

Once upon a time there was a shop. Not that you ever went in it. But it was definitely there. What did it sell? Key fobs? Cloths? Colanders? You feel sure it was something old-fashioned. Maybe you'll look it up on Google Street View later, move the little man around and see what it was. Like being a time-traveller, going back three weeks.

Because now it's gone, it's not there any more. Well, the shop is there. The building, the walls, the window. But what was in the shop that's gone? Glue? Hammers? Bath plugs? And what about the man who worked there? He's gone too. (You did go in there once to get – what was it? A book? A pond lining? Toothpaste? – and the man seemed very nice, but you didn't get it there because you found it cheaper online.)

There's nothing there now. Well, not nothing. The window is covered with a big poster that promises something better than an old shop selling string or grapes or buckets, something that promises to change the very fabric of society itself, because, it says:

215

EXCITING NEW CONCEPT COMING SOON

What can this new concept be, you think? This new concept in shops? It sounds like it's truly groundbreaking. Will it be a shop that has no gravity? A shop that works out what you already own but have forgotten about and tries to sell it to you again? Will it be a shop staffed by ghosts?

The truth is, it will be a shop that is just that: a shop. It will sell trousers or phones or cheese or something. The 'exciting concept' will be that it has iPads you can look at, or its entire staff wears dungarees, or it's got really loud music in it. It will just be a shop.

Because there haven't been many truly 'exciting' new concepts in the history of retail. Selfridge's, perhaps – the first department store, with everything under one roof. Or the first supermarkets in the 1930s – the first 'self-service' shops. But really they were just variations on the theme of 'come in, buy something, leave'.

In fact, the promise of something really exciting in the world of retail is probably something to be feared rather than keenly anticipated. The only truly unique retail 'concept' that has ever really got any traction is Argos – the shop where you have to do a small amount of paperwork to get your goods. And that's not a concept that anyone would really describe as 'sexy'.

But it's not going to be an Argos where the old shop was (What was it? Flowers? Fish? Frisbees?). The space is too small, the location too unfavourable. It's probably, looking at the shops on either side, going to be exactly the same as them.

The trouble is, right now you really need to buy a pint of milk and there's nowhere to get . . . hang on, that's it, it was a corner shop! It sold *everything*. Now you'll have to walk to the supermarket. The shop where you used to buy milk is now a concept and a concept won't help you make a cup of tea. Unless, of course, the exciting new concept is just that – a shop that sells nothing but pints and pints of milk. That's not just a shop, that's a contender for the Turner Prize, and as concepts go, that really is rather exciting.

Lies to watch out for from . . .
Couples wanting to get married

LIE # **66**

" *Yes, we believe in God.* "

Believing in God has its uses. For the poor and the dispossessed, the promise of eternal paradise tomorrow stops the revolution from happening today. For those who've lost a loved one, the possibility of some future meeting is balm for the broken heart. And for a couple of atheists hoping to have a church wedding it ticks a lot of boxes.

It's curious how many non-believers want to get married in church. It's most likely a matter of architecture. Nothing says 'We're officially hitched!' like a photograph of a beaming couple stood by a very old door; nothing gives a marriage gravitas like signing a register in a vestry that smells of damp and doubt.

The 'Yes, we believe in God' lie is so clearly a lie it requires proof, and this can take months to provide. First of all, the non-believers must meet with the vicar of the church that offers the best photo opportunities. This in itself is a nerve-wracking experience. As the not-yet-weds walk the church path for the first time they feel like Damien from *The Omen*. Over a cup of tea the vicar tells them he expects to see them every week, and so the merry dance begins.

Every Sunday they stand at the back mouthing along to the boring old tunes; pretending to read the hymn book while secretly looking at Twitter. After the service they smile and feign enlightenment, before loading the collection plate with coins they would prefer to spend in the pub.

On the day of the wedding the sun comes out and all of their friends gather in the shade. We won't be getting married in a church they tell each other, but most of them will. In the pews the congregation gets the giggles. The organ sounds so stupid and why does the vicar speak like that? He tells the congregation how he's got to know the happy couple over the last few months and makes a joke about Spurs. Parents smile proudly, friends pinch themselves and look at the floor. The readings are bemusing to most and the hymns sound like the lows of wounded cows. One man sings too loudly, others not at all.

Rings on fingers they stand by the old door and get the pictures they came for. The vicar says he's looking forward to seeing them after the honeymoon. They thank him for a beautiful day.

A year later they bump into the vicar in a chip shop. It's odd seeing him here, so out of context. Like finding an egg in your shoe. They would have come back but work has been very busy and now she's pregnant it's not so easy. He understands. He understands everything.

Years later they find themselves sitting on some tiny chairs in front of a blackboard. 'Yes, we believe in God,' they tell the headmaster. We used to go to St Giles all the time, got married there in fact, but we've fallen out of step with attendance of late. And here they go again, telling the same old lie to someone else who has heard it all before.

LIE # **67**

"Excuse me, I need the loo."

So you've been talking to this person at a party for what seems like an age and you can't think of any other way of ending the conversation.

It's not that they are boring, per se; it's just that you don't really know each other very well. You've said everything that two strangers at a party who don't want to get off with each other can say.

They're probably thinking the same thing. They're trying to think of a way of ending it as well. Not ending it all, not suicide – just ending the conversation.

But no one else seems to be joining you. It occurs to you that one of you – you? him? – must have a reputation for being boring. No one wants to join you in case you decide to leg it and leave them alone with him. Or is it you that no one wants to talk to?

There's no one near enough to lure into your web. This conversation could, on paper, go on for ever.

And you're having to work all this out while talking to them, while making your mouth make sounds and making your head and ears do movements that indicate that you are somehow listening to and comprehending the sounds that their mouth is making.

How to stop it? Do you do the confident thing that's happened to you before? Do you just say: 'Well, great to chat? Better mingle.' When people have said that to you, you've respected them. Admired them even. It seems a strong move. But you're not sure you can do it, can say it without it looking mean. It's too bold a move for you.

What's your other option? Get another drink? You haven't finished this one yet. Knock it back. Gulp it back then go and get another one. Most natural thing in the world.

[*Keep nodding; keep saying sounds.*]

But then – you'll have to offer them a drink. You try and look at their glass. Is it full or empty? It's empty. You'll have to offer to get them a drink. And then get it. And then come back. And then you'll be exactly where you are right now. Stuck in this pedestrian conversation.

(Here's a secret party strategy for what you should do in this situation. Use the Three Drinks Ploy: Ask if they want a drink. Go and get it from the kitchen or the bar or whatever. Here's the smart part – when you come back, come back with three drinks. Give them their one, then sort of make a face that indicates that you need to give the third drink to someone else.

A further elaboration on this ploy is to always carry two drinks with you at a party – one you're actually drinking, one that's untouched. If trapped with someone you don't want to talk to, say, 'I'd better get this to Jeff/

Naomi/Paul', and then you can go. It's the perfect technique for escaping any conversation you don't want to be a part of.)

But just while you're pondering this, someone comes round and *fills your glasses*. Now what are you going to do?

What to talk about next? Horses? Drums? Guesthouses? E. E. Cummings? Was that a pause in which to escape? Oh no, not a pause.

OK, there's nothing for it. It's your last resort. Going to the loo.

Do you actually need the loo? No. But it's your only way out.

Why is it always you? Why doesn't he say he needs the loo? Don't tell me he's actually enjoying this conversation? He really must be the boring one, if this is his idea of a good time.

No, you're going to have to do it.

'You'll have to excuse me, I need the loo.'

'OK,' he says. He's won. He knows it. You blinked first. You're chicken.

You head towards the loo. For the first time in half an hour you can think clearly. You wait in the queue. You go in. You pretend to have a wee.

And then you come out.

And bang straight into him again.

'Ah,' he says, 'Now where were we?'

LIE # 68

"I'm six foot"
and other online dating lies

It used to be impossible to lie about your height to a prospective partner because the first time you ever made contact with them would have to be, embarrassingly, in person.

In person, you can lie about lots of things to a potential lover – your real name, the fact that you already have a partner, your reasons for being in a lay-by on the M26 at midnight – but height is not one of them. (Unless you meet somewhere where you remain permanently seated, like a session of the UN Security Council, although romantic hook-ups during emergency meetings on Syria are, we're told, rare.)

However, online dating means that for the first time, it is possible to lie to a prospective life partner from the off. From before you've even met them. Start as you mean to go on!

So it comes as little surprise that a recent study found that the number-one most common lie on an online-dating profile was about height, with many male online daters adding at least an inch or two (to their height).

This is, to a degree, understandable. Suppose you're a guy whose height is hovering just below the magical six feet. Your prospective bride might have set her search requirements for someone over six foot, meaning she would miss out on ever seeing your handsome face. Really you're doing *her* a favour by letting her see you in her results page.

But while understandable, it's also fraught with risks. The main one being that she'll notice when you actually meet her and think that you're a habitual dissembler who she probably shouldn't share the rest of her life with.

Most men bank on the fact that she won't notice – who can judge how tall six foot is, exactly? (Except for maybe a six-foot woman looking for a tall partner – and she's too tall for you anyway.) It's not like women carry a tape measure around with them. And anyway, you can always try sitting down for a lot of your first date – you'll be in a bar or a restaurant or a permanent session of the UN Security Council or something. And whatever, when she meets you she'll forget about your height because she'll be so dazzled by your looks, your physique and your life.

But the trouble is you probably lied about those things as well. Because here's the rest of the list of the study's top ten online-dating lies, told by men and women.

2. Age
You can get away with taking a couple of years off, even if you meet someone, but what is the impression you're

giving – would you rather be thought of as a fresh-looking forty-year-old? Or a haggard thirty-year-old?

3. Weight

Like height, this is a lie that people think they can get away with even though they are meeting someone and it's the first thing they will notice. It's mainly told by women who are hoping that, while men might say they want a skinny girlfriend, they *actually* want a fuller-figured one. It's a theory.

4. Income

Men commonly add between 20 and 40 per cent to their income. This is pretty easy to lie about and get away with – for an hour or two. Yes, you can try to woo your date with dinner at an expensive restaurant. But when she comes home with you and discovers that you live in a bedsit in north Wembley, she might start to suspect the truth.

5. Job

This might not be an outright lie, more a reimagining of an actual job. Are you actually head of sales for an international telecommunications company? Or do you sell phone cards from a booth near the station?

6. Physique

Many men describe themselves as 'athletic'. And they might not be consciously lying. After all, sumo wrestlers are athletes.

7. Photographs

People lie a little here by putting up pictures that have been taken in near darkness, or even Photoshopped. They tend not to put up pictures of totally different people. That would make recognising each other in a bar difficult: 'I think you're expecting me?' 'No, I'm waiting for Lenny Kravitz.'

8. Lifestyle

What is lifestyle? What does it mean? No one knows. And that's why people are forced to lie about it. If you say you have 'a lifestyle', it means you don't know what it means, and you don't have one.

9. Hobbies and interests

Do you really like to go base-jumping? It does sound a lot sexier than 'eating a Morrison's ready-meal in front of *Game of Thrones*'.

10. Connections to celebrities

Of all people, 3.3 per cent say that they have connections to celebrities when they actually don't. Why? Connections to celebrities don't impress people, as I was saying to Simon Le Bon the other day. Yes, *that* Simon Le Bon.

If you weren't happily married men, do you think you would ever consider online dating? And if so, would you lie on your profile?

David:

Well on Facebook, I'm a thirteen-year-old girl.

Lee:

And I'm massive on Grinder. Massive. And the fibs I've been telling! I'm not even close by. I just leave my phone at a station and then watch their faces as they look around at a mannequin.

David:

Same here. I'm on Grinder with a different face and a different name, and in fact, if they go for the date that guy actually turns up. That's how much of a lie it is.

LIE # 68

" Would I lie to you? "

'If I find out you've been having an affair it's over!'

'Would I lie to you, darling?'

'How can you say that, after Sandra?'

'That was different.'

'Why?'

'I was nine.'

'Can I trust you?'

'Of course you can. I'd never lie to you.'

'Yeah but if I find out you *have* lied to me I'll never be able to trust you again. That's the problem with saying "would I lie to you?"'

'I know.'

'So don't say it.'

'But I'm not lying.'

'You said that about Sandra.'

'I was *nine*.'

'The truth is the truth, Moffat.'

'Truth is a matter of perception.'

'Stop being all clever-clever.'

'You don't like it when I'm all clever-clever, do you?'

'It frightens me. You know I can't do clever-clever.'

'I promise it won't happen again.'

'Stop promising stuff.'

'Sorry.'

'So?'

'So what?'

'Have you been having an affair?'

'Of course not.'

'Swear on your mother's life.'

'I've not been having an affair.'

'You didn't do it.'

'Do what?'

'Swear on your mother's life.'

'I don't like being manipulated.'

'And I don't like it when my husband has sex with other women.'

'I've already told you, there is no affair.'

'Swear it then.'

'I swear on my mother's life that I haven't been having an affair.'

'Let me see your hands.'

'What?'

'Your hands are behind your back. You're probably crossing your fingers!'

'This is ridiculous.'

'Do it again, with your hands out front. Go.'

'I swear that I haven't been having an affair.'

'Add the mother bit.'

'I don't want to.'

'DO IT.'

230

'I swear on my mother's life that I haven't had sexual relations with another woman.'

'You changed it!'

'No, I didn't.'

'You changed it to a Clinton. You did a Clinton. That's what he said.'

'What did he say?'

'"*Sexual relations*".'

'Did he?'

'You know he did.'

'Nope.'

'You're such a liar.'

'I've already told you, I'd never lie to you.'

'It doesn't matter anyway . . . I *know* you're having an affair.'

'No I'm not . . . Who told you?'

'Nigel told me.'

'*Nigel*?'

'Nigel.'

'Nigel's a git.'

'He's not, he's a very generous lover.'

'Hold on – *you're* having an affair? With *Nigel*?'

'Yes.'

'That's not very nice of you is it?'

'I guess it's not. I'm sorry.'

'I'm sorry too.'

'Kiss?'

'Lay it on me.'

LIE # 70

"I'm sorry, but someone's actually sitting there."

This is one of the great pub lies we've all told or been told at some point in our pathetic little lives. Picture the scene. It's a winter's night. Let's say it's a Tuesday. It's a rainy Tuesday night and you've decided to meet a couple of friends after work for a drink and a good old bitch about Jane or Dan or Chris or Sylvester or whoever it happens to be who's rubbing you up the wrong way this week.

You arrive first in the pub. It's a fancy place. It used to be an old man's pub, but now it's called something like The Retreating Wimpole or Not a Florist's. They serve burgers on roof tiles and sell craft beers. The staff have funny-coloured hair and tattoos. Some of them like to smoke roll-ups in the pub garden while they regret going to art college. You feel for them, after all they could be you. But thankfully they're not. You don't work in a pub. You work in an office with Jane and Dan and Chris and Sylvester, who it just so happens have really been getting your goat this week.

You arrive at the pub first and look for a table. It's only 7 p.m. but it's already busy. There's a postman, who looks

232

very drunk, shouting in his friend's ear; a couple kissing by the fire (almost certainly having an affair); and a very old man wondering where the pool table has gone and why it's been replaced by a vintage armchair and a milking stool. Over by the loos you spot the only empty table and make a dash for it. You quickly take a seat. There are two other chairs, so you put your coat on one and your bag on another. Great, you're settled. Only you haven't got a drink yet and you don't want to risk going to the bar and leaving your valuables unattended. Last time you did that someone nicked your laptop which had some randy photos on it. You go red just at the memory.

A couple appear in front of you, clearly in search of seats. They whisper something to each other and then he steps forward. 'Excuse me,' he says 'Do you mind if we . . .' He waves his arm between the two chairs next to you. And that's when you lie. You don't even think about it, it just slips right out, easy as pie. 'I'm sorry,' you say, 'but someone's actually sitting there.'

The man looks annoyed. So does his girlfriend. You are clearly alone. He cranes his neck about the pub exaggeratedly looking for your absent companions; his girlfriend sips her stupid wine. But you hold firm. 'They've just gone to the . . .' You trail off. Gone where? To the circus? Prison? To interview Boris Becker? You take your phone out of your bag and start skimming through emails like you're an important person who has nothing to add to this conversation. But they don't move. They

233

stand awkwardly close to the table sniping about you and pointing at the empty chairs.

A minute passes and soon becomes five. You realise that the sniping couple are still talking about you. Whatever else they came to the pub to chat about has long been forgotten. They have just one thing on their minds – you and your refusal to give up the empty seats. You take a sip from the drink you don't have and scan the bar, desperate for a glimpse of your late arrivals.

The pub door swings open and you heave a sigh of relief. But it's premature, for in shuffles a middle-aged man with what appears to be a broken foot. It's covered in plaster up to just beneath the toes and has a sort of blue rubber bung for a heel. His digits look purple and squashed, like somebody dropped a snooker table on them. The nail of his big toe is completely black. It reminds you of a tinted window.

The sniping couple have stopped sniping and now flick looks between you and the invalid at the door. They seem to be smiling for the first time since they arrived. You make a show of pretending to look for something in your trouser pockets; it's as if you're hoping to find your friends there.

You look up to see that Broken Foot Man is holding the door open for somebody else, and seconds later the tapping stick of his elderly companion tip-taps its hesitant entry over the threshold. The hand that grips the stick looks positively prehistoric, almost like a claw. The skin is translucent and the veins beneath are thick smudges of purple and blue. The hand belongs to the oldest man you have ever seen. He's nothing more than a collection of dust in a jumper. He moves with the gait of a man trying to straddle a barrel, and wheezes like an overfull Hoover bag.

There is only one thing to do. You grab your phone and have an imaginary conversation with absolutely no one. You nod and gesticulate with the plausibility of an extra in the Queen Vic, hoping to convey to any onlookers that the news from the other end relates to some sort of crisis. You stand (still in pretend phone conversation mode) and roll your eyes at the sniping couple as if to say 'You'll never believe what's just happened' while simultaneously gesturing to the new arrivals that your table is now free. You grab your things and slip out into the darkening night.

Once outside you text your friends and ask their whereabouts. There's been a mix-up and they are in a different pub, The Fractious Ghost, just around the corner. You say you are on your way but they tell you not to bother, there's nowhere at all to sit. You buy a microwave meal and get the bus home. There's nowhere to sit on the bus, well there is, but that would mean asking somebody to move their bag, and right now that's not a conversation you feel like having.

LIE # 71

66 I've lost my phone. 99

Hello, is that customer service? Hello, yes, here's my customer number.

I'm ringing on the landline because I've lost my mobile phone.

And I definitely haven't just dropped it down the toilet.

Yes, I've lost it. I'm not sure where – that's the thing about losing something isn't it? If you knew where you'd lost it then you'd know where it is. And I don't know where my phone is.

It definitely isn't sitting in a bowl of rice in the kitchen right now.

Hmm . . . Yes, sorry can't be more helpful than that. I might have lost it on the Tube. Or not on the Tube. I'm not sure.

I'm definitely not looking at it now.

What do you mean? My policy doesn't cover me for loss? What does that mean?

I mean I have lost it, sort of. In the sense that it's lost any functionality since it fell in the loo. Which it didn't.

So, I can only get a new one if it was stolen. Well, I

guess . . . I guess it was stolen. It must have been stolen. Because there's no way I could have lost it if it wasn't stolen.

I hope that it still isn't sending out some sort of signal.

Yes, it must have been stolen. Stolen by a pickpocket, I guess. Or a professional phone stealer. I hear there's a lot of it about. From abroad. Professionals. Someone like me has no chance. Yes, it must have been stolen from me at some point yesterday. Or today. I'm not sure where.

I need to get a crime number from the police? Well, OK. OK. I can do that. That's no problem; I can call the police and tell them it's been stolen. I mean, it has been stolen, so that's the right thing to do.

It has sort of been stolen. Stolen from me. By water. And rice.

So, right, I just call the police and tell them that it's been stolen and then they'll give me a number and you'll get me a new phone? A newer one? Oh, the same one. Even if it's been stolen?

Is it a crime to report a crime that didn't happen? It sounds like a crime. But is it a massive crime? It's not like armed robbery or murder. Surely the police won't arrest me for this? I do get a new phone out of it – it's no skin off their nose. I bet the coppers do this sort of thing all the time. I bet they never have to buy a new phone.

OK, well I'll do all of that and then call back. Because my phone is definitely broken, I mean lost, I mean stolen.

LIE # 72

" I got you a voucher so that you can get yourself something you really want. "

A present says a lot about the person who gives it, and nothing says 'I couldn't be bothered to spend more than five minutes thinking about your birthday' than a gift voucher. Some people try to pretend that a voucher isn't a voucher by wrapping it in pretty paper and tying a ribbon on top. Never do this. It's like serving a meal of cat poo and cold potatoes on a well-laid table. Your friend will notice, and it leaves a bad taste in the mouth. Nothing hurts the birthday boy more than tearing off the paper from a decent looking present only to find a £15 voucher for a camping shop inside.

Everything about the voucher is wrong. It immediately creates work for the person unlucky enough to receive it. They either have to hop online and navigate their way through a complicated series of clicks, ticks and access codes, or venture into town and find the actual shop before the chit expires. Having found the shop (Expert Camper! Why does Jill think I like camping?) they discover there's nothing on sale for the value of the coupon and end up putting their hand in their own pocket to supplement the purchase (in this case, a crampon. It's still under the bed in the spare room, Jill). Alternatively, the voucher sits unused in the purse or wallet only to be discovered five years after the shop went bust or your interest in, say, camping, waned or never began.

Some people dispense with the voucher altogether and just give cold, hard cash. In the case of grandparents this is often sellotaped to the inside of a birthday card along with a Rich Tea biscuit they mistook for a fifty-pence piece. Here it's less a case of thoughtlessness and more a case of that's what grandparents do, and we rather like it. But when your brother fishes in his pocket and presents you with a crumpled twenty-pound note and a card from the petrol station, the charm is somewhat lost.

The trick to avoiding the gift voucher is to let people know precisely what you want for at least six months before your birthday. Blog about it, tweet about it, hand them magazines with things you desire circled in red. Call them from a withheld number at three in the morning and whisper menacingly into the phone: 'John would like a Swingball for his birthday. Failing that, new headphones.' But whatever you do, never assume that people have got the measure of your tastes, and never feign interest in a present that disappoints. I can't stress this last point enough. Polite approval of an unwanted gift can lead to a different sort of present pain, and here's how.

It's your ninth birthday and your aunt is thinking

about what to buy you. She has a vague memory of you once pointing at a pig as you drove past a farm together so she buys you a small cuddly pig toy. She gives it to you on your birthday, and despite not really understanding why, you smile, cuddle it for a bit, and then chuck it on top of a cupboard. For your tenth birthday, the same aunt remembers that you seemed to like the pig she gave you last year so she buys you another one. It's got a slightly different snout, but to all intents and purposes it's another cuddly pig. You politely smile as you unwrap it, jiggle it about for a bit, and then, when she's gone, sling it on top of the cupboard with the other one. You now have two pigs on top of your cupboard. Anybody passing by might think you were starting a pig collection. The next year, what with you being a bit old for cuddly toys, your aunt gives you a pig mug. It's funny because it's pink and looks a bit like a snout. You smile as you unwrap it and make a point of drinking some squash from it before she leaves. Other people at the party notice you drinking from your pig mug and remember the two pigs on top of your cupboard. The next year, everybody buys you something pig related. You get pig badges, pig books, coasters with pigs on, jigsaws of pigs, piggy-shaped biscuits and piggy-shaped soap. You now have a sizeable pig collection and over the years it grows and grows as people bring you pig tat back from all corners of the globe. Christmas, birthdays and holiday gifts all add to your haul, until one day you find yourself sat on *The One Show* sofa discussing your pig collection with Matt Baker and Alex Jones while nervously patting the head of a flustered sow they've brought into the studio for a laugh. And all because you didn't have the heart to tell your aunt you didn't want her silly pig present in the first place.

Next time it's your turn to buy someone a gift, remember that what you give speaks volumes about *you*. The perfect present should show that you are interesting, cultured, thoughtful, witty, generous and a lover of quality. Should you fail to find anything to fit that bill, might I recommend the *Would I Lie To You?* book, available from all good retailers, £14.99

LIE # 73

" We don't watch TV. "

Of all the lies told to you by people at parties, this is the most annoying. You're talking to some bloke you've never met before in your life. You've gone through how you know the host and how you got there and what the nibbles are like. You're thinking of an exit plan. You decide, as a last throw of the dice, to talk about something you saw on TV last night. And instead of being met either with interest, ignorance or indifference, you receive a polemic. Almost a telling-off for watching TV.

'We don't watch TV,' he says. 'We don't even have a TV.'

He's disgusted with you. He hates you. He thinks you have a brain the size of a pituitary gland. Because in his head, all TV is bad. He thinks you're sitting there in your pants all day watching *All-Star Family Fortunes* and *Flog It!* and *Geordie Shore* and *The Great British Bake-Off* and *Final Score* and fun stuff like that. It doesn't occur to him that a lot of television is documentaries about the Incas or CERN or the situation in Syria.

He wants you to know that he thinks you are an idiot. A disgusting idiot. A dolt. A worker ant. Someone who has taken the establishment bait and sits in a narcoleptic stupor all evening, blind to the plight of the world, injecting yourself with the drug of TV.

But who is he to think that he's so good? So virtuous? Why has he decided the right thing to do is banish television – the medium that changed the world, a medium that can inform, educate and entertain, a medium that *everyone* likes? What makes him think that not having a TV is a good idea? Isn't that like someone saying 'we don't have the internet'? Or saying in the eighteenth century, 'we don't read newspapers'? Or books? Or letters? Or in the nineteenth century saying, 'we don't look at telegrams; we won't have a telegram in the house'? Doesn't it make you a fool not to be connected to the world with the latest method of communication?

Of course, you don't mention this when you're talking. You act all polite. Even though he's been rude. You act all: 'So sorry to have bored you with my trivial life, it must be so tedious for a superhuman like yourself to even have to hear my breath.'

You say: 'Oh, you don't have a TV. How wonderful!' Not 'how weird' or 'how ridiculous' or 'how boring'.

And then, since you can see the glee in their eyes, you give them the chance to expand on their anachronistic theories.

'No telly,' you say. 'So you don't watch anything?'

And then the truth comes out.

'Well,' they say, 'I mean, we watched *Wolf Hall* on the

laptop. But that's only because we'd read the book.'

(Who is this 'we' he keeps talking about? He seems too pompous to have a partner.)

'And occasionally we watch *The Apprentice* on iPlayer. For a laugh. And we've seen all of *Breaking Bad* on DVD. It's amazing. More like a film than a TV programme. And we've got Netflix so we can watch *House of Cards*. Which is brilliant. And we've really got into *Borgen*. Which is not in English, so more our cup of tea.'

'But you don't have a TV?' you say. 'You watch it all on a computer?'

'Well . . .' he admits, cracking under your Gestapo-like interrogation. 'We do have a TV in the little room. But not the main living room.' (Where he never spends any time.)

'Yeah, we got a 45-inch plasma to watch the Six Nations on. And the golf. And the racing. And *Top Gear*. But we never channel surf. We only watch things that we've circled in the *Telegraph* listings magazine.'

So he does watch TV; he does *have* a TV.

'So you *do* watch TV?'

'No. We don't watch TV,' he says.

'OK,' you say. 'Right, time for another drink.'

And off you wander, in search of more Prosecco and fewer bores.

Do you ever meet people who claim that they don't watch TV?

Lee:

I get it. People say to me: 'I like your show. I actually don't watch much telly.' As if to go: 'Just don't think of me as one of these people that watches *anything*. I don't watch *anything*. I mean, I'd still watch your show despite the fact that I despise the world you work in.'

Rob:

I think it's a class thing. If I'm ever at a thing and there's a lot of posh people, that's where it's most likely they'll say, 'Oh, so and so told me you were on the telly, but I don't watch it.'

David:

Then they say, 'I'm so sorry, I just don't watch much television, I don't have time, but apparently you matter in some way, though I don't really buy into all that nonsense.'

LIE # 74

"Yes, everything was fine thanks. "

As we sit in a restaurant at the end of a meal, stuffed full of sausage and treacle tart, wired on coffee and giddy with wine, the time comes when we have to settle up. We catch a waiter's eye and make the universal mime of signing our name in the air. Moments later, he presents us with a bill secreted in some sort of oversized wallet, and a bowl of mints. He smiles and asks us if everything was all right with the meal, but it's an empty question. For every waiter in the world knows that unless they actually dropped their trousers at the table and took a crap in your salad nobody ever complains. We might moan about the food and bitch about the service behind their backs, but when it comes to paying the bill we all cough up saying, 'Yes, everything was fine, thanks', and leave a healthy tip.

If we weren't all so frightened of confrontation we might take this opportunity to say what we really think. Things like:

I was a little disappointed that we were sat under the noisy air-conditioning unit. It made it very difficult

246

for my date to hear the punchlines to all my brilliant jokes and it blew with such ferocity that I dined in a scarf.

I would have preferred it if you hadn't been scratching your belly as you talked me through the additional pizza toppings.

Do you always bring people's meals at different times? It felt odd to be eating my ice cream while Martin was still waiting for his soup.

Watching the chef smoke by the bins tempered my enjoyment of the fish.

Are cold chips the house style?

It was a shame I had to wait so long for a refill because the waiter had gone outside to inspect his friend's new motorbike.

I'm not that interested in listening to the staff discussing next week's shift rota and arguing about whose turn it is to check the toilets.

There was a dirty plaster in my noodles.

Why do you choose to wash only some of the cutlery?

I know it wasn't particularly busy tonight, but perhaps the staff could think of other things to do than crowd around an iPad watching Dapper Laughs.

*I swear I saw a dog through the kitchen door pawing a
couple of saucepans.*

*The moussaka was so nuclear hot from the microwave
it removed the roof of my friend's mouth.*

I prefer my banana fritters to be hair free.

We *might* take this opportunity but we don't. And restaurants are so sure that we won't they've already added the tip to the bill. It's an aggressive move but a profitable one. The withholding of a tip was once our last chance to protest and we enjoyed taking it. 'Well, I won't be leaving a tip' we'd say to our fellow diners; 'They can think again if they think I'm giving them a tip for that!' And we'd hurriedly put our coats on and leg it out of the door before the staff realised. But now the restaurant has taken back control and asks us to tell them if we want the tip removed. As if that's ever going to happen. If we're not prepared to complain that somebody sneezed in the mash then we're certainly not going to quibble about the additional 10 per cent. So instead we suck on the complimentary mint, give the waiter our weakest smile and say, 'Yes, everything was fine, thanks.'

66 *My lips are sealed.* **99**

Pssst. Do you want to know a secret? Promise you won't tell anyone else? You see I said I wouldn't say anything to anyone, but seeing as it's you, I'll make an exception. Ready? Right, here goes:

(*Checks to see who else is around then leans in conspiratorially*)

When people say 'My lips are sealed' they are almost always lying.

You're kidding?

I'm not.

I don't believe it.

It's true.

Who told you?

Mark.

When did you see Mark?

Last night. I saw him coming out of Jenny's house so I waved and we just got talking.

What was he doing at Jenny's house?

I dunno, but he looked well embarrassed that I'd seen him. Don't say anything will you?

Course not. Does Paul know he was round there?

No, Paul's gone to visit his mum. Well, that's what he told Jen, but I saw Claire at the weekend and she said she'd seen Paul out with Sarah, so I'm not sure where he's gone. Don't say anything to anyone will you? I promised Claire I wouldn't mention it, but I might as well tell you.

No, I won't say anything, course I won't. Anyway, from what I hear Claire's not little miss perfect.

How come?

Oh, Del told me she's been seeing John again, but Tim has no idea.

You're kidding!

I'm not. But don't tell anyone will you? I promised Del I wouldn't say anything, but as it's you, it seems daft not to.

Thanks.

You're welcome.

So what else do you know?

Not much really. Well, quite a lot actually. But I can't say.

Oh come on, you can't leave it like that. I won't say anything.

Promise?

Promise.

I think I'm pregnant.

You're kidding! That's amazing news.

Don't tell anyone. I've not told anyone and I want to wait a bit until I'm sure.

Of course I won't say anything. My lips are sealed. That's great news!

I know. I can't believe it. I've not even told Chris yet. Right, I best get back. See you later.

(She leaves; someone else sits down. A brief silence, then . . .)

You'll never guess who's pregnant?

251

LIE # **76**

Till death us do part

Look at your bride. Damn, she's hot. If only the air-con was working! But even with that thin sheen of sweat on her forehead you still love her loads. You are so happy. This is the best day of your life. Someone should kill you now! (Perhaps Gareth will, he's always had a thing for Meg.)

You said 'Till death do us part' and you meant it, along with all the other bits ('in sickness and in health', 'for richer for poorer', 'sorry, Vicar'). You're off on your honeymoon in forty minutes. That should be fun – you've never been to Chelmsford before.

Hold on, though. Nearly half of all UK marriages end in divorce. Someone's telling porkies.

'Not me!' you respond quickly. 'I meant every word of it!'

'Everyone feels that way at the start,' they counter. 'The best-laid schemes o' mice an' men.'

'Mice and men? Sorry, mate, don't know what you're talking about.'

Love is a flighty mistress. She comes, she goes; she

comes back, she exits for good and slams the door on your toes. You cry but she doesn't care. The ripest of beginnings may crumble to dust. Dreams die. Beauty fades. Life is cruel. Get used to it.

'Not us,' you say. 'I can't imagine not loving this woman. Eh, Meg?'

'Definitely,' says Meg. 'My love for you is so strong. When we started courting I had a small crush on Gareth but that burnt itself out quickly enough, especially when he was transferred abroad. In fact, I think it helped bring us together.'

'You had a crush on Gareth?'

What are the chances that you'll get over the finishing line together? You hope that you'll stick at it but you can't be sure. Life creeps up on us, people change, cars break down.

'Define crush,' you say.

'It was nothing. I just liked his bottom.'

'His bottom?'

'It's firm.'

'What's wrong with my bottom?'

'Nothing. I love its crinkle effect.'

'But you prefer Gareth's?'

'I never said "prefer". I like them in different ways.'

'You still like his bottom?'

'Only from afar.'

'Oh, this is great, this is.'

How many of us truly believe that when it comes to marriage, life means life? Perhaps we did once, but no longer. In today's market a better offer is only a right-swipe away.

'OK, I don't like his bottom.'

'You already said you did.'

'Darling, you're the one I've married.'

'Why don't you and Gareth's bottom run away together? I'm sure you and the bottom will be very happy.'

'This is ridiculous, I've never even seen his bottom.'

'You'd like to though, wouldn't you?'

'No.'

'Yes, you would!'

'OK! I would! I would like to see his bottom! Is that what you want to hear?'

'I knew it!'

'You're a twit.'

'You're welcome to the bottom.'

'And what's that supposed to mean?'

'It's over, Meg.'

'What do you mean?'

'I can't be married to a woman who'd rather live with a bottom.'

'Fair enough. See you later, then.'

'I'll Facebook you.'

Lies to watch out for from . . . **Luvvies**

LIE # **77**

" *I haven't prepared a speech,*
because I really didn't think
I was going to win. **"**

There's nothing we like to see more than an actor on a red carpet, unless the red of the carpet is blood and the actor is on their back having fallen out of a loft hatch. But usually, where there's a red carpet there's an award ceremony round the corner where gongs will be given and tears will be shed.

The lowlight of all these glittering prize fests is the speeches. These tend to fall into distinct categories, each as painful to witness as the rest, and each detailed below.

The 'thank absolutely everyone' speech:

Some gushing idiot who has just picked up an award for playing, I dunno, the inventor of chewing gum, takes it upon himself to thank every single person he has have ever met. The list goes on for ever as he names people we've never heard of; like a local dignitary reading a roll call of those killed in a mining disaster.

The 'crying so much I can't actually speak' speech:

Were it not for the fun of watching snot streak the make-up of a Hollywood beauty, this blub-a-thank would have us reaching for our remote controls. Instead, we watch through our fingers as an overpaid sniveller weeps and wails like a child who's dropped their lolly at the zoo.

The 'stumble and mumble while looking at the floor' speech:

'I'd like to thank, er . . . Oh God, I'm not very good at this, um, I'd like to thank . . . where's Tom? Is Tom here? No? Oh well, if Tom was here he'd remember that time on set when, er, that funny thing happened . . .'

The 'over-rehearsed script with jokes that nobody laughs at' speech:

No matter how deafening the silence where the laughs should be, this winner has rehearsed so hard there is absolutely no way they can cut it short or change anything. So a room full of the great and the overpaid curl their toes as a visual FX supervisor tells another 'joke' about a green-screen mix-up.

But bad as these all may be, nothing irks quite as much as the luvvie that takes to the stage and utters the big fat lie:

'I haven't prepared a speech, because I really didn't think I was going to win.'

What do they mean, they didn't think they were going to win? They are in a category of four nominees. And it's not like they haven't seen award ceremonies before where the result was unexpected. Of course they thought they might win, and of course they spent the whole week leading up to the ceremony rehearsing their speech again and again – in the shower; on the loo; walking up the stairs; walking down the stairs; staring in the fridge; squeezing their teabags; moisturising; doing their press-ups; taking out the recycling; changing a light bulb; chopping onions; flossing; tossing their socks in the laundry bin; loading the dishwasher; turning lights off; turning lights on; drawing the curtains; sniffing the milk – so you'd have thought they would have got it down pat by now. And you know what, they have. Because the speech they've been endlessly rehearsing was simply this:

'I haven't prepared a speech, because I really didn't think I was going to win.'

Liars.

LIE # 78

66"You were great!"99

You're in a relationship. Well done! We knew you'd find someone. Unfortunately, your partner is a little uncertain about themselves in key areas (work, the bedroom, appearance and driving). Luckily, you're there to reassure them. Why? Because you're a team!

Being in a team means always saying, 'You were great!' In modern parlance this is a 'bigging-up' of your partner, a way of boosting their fragile ego, which shows few signs of resilience despite years of psychotherapy.

Take last week. Your boyfriend was nervous, forgetful and stuttery. Frankly, you weren't sure you'd ever want to sleep with him again! But by telling him he was great he thought he *was* great and in time could *become* great. It's an incredible trick, one that was invented by The Magic Circle in 1902.

And remember the best man speech he gave last year? Man that was the pits. You told him *twice* not to tell the nun joke he pulled off the internet, but he did it anyway. Everyone went quiet, save for Gerald who did the fake laugh. Then he panicked and missed a big chunk out. But afterwards, when he looked like a lost school-boy, you told him he was great. And you know what? He perked up! 'You were right,' he said later, tie loose and at a jaunty angle. 'On reflection I *was* great!' You smiled and kissed him. Your work was done. Although you felt a residual frustration, probably because he really had been rubbish and not acknowledged it. But you can't have it both ways.

Something similar happened when he did that brass rubbing of Harold the Unpleasant. Word got around and he received the call from BBC Radio Gerrards Cross. This is what he'd been working towards all his life. On the day he was keyed up. 'You'll be great,' you told him, trying to boost his self-confidence in advance of the event.

You tuned in live. His voice broke and he burped, all within the first nine seconds. He then sneezed, shouted and mooed. The presenter asked a question about the best conditions to rub brass. He answered, before breaking down in tears. At the end he sang two verses of 'Suburbia' by the Pet Shop Boys, then signed off in Chinese.

Back home you reassured him. 'You were great!' you told him. 'People love to hear real emotion and cow sounds on local radio.' 'Really?' he replied. '*Really,*' you said. 'You were right,' he told you later. 'I was great. Really great, in fact.' You smiled, and a part of you died.

But there's a problem. What if he spots the pattern of you telling him he's great when he's not? You're in trouble then, because the spell is broken: 'If you always tell me I'm great even when I'm not, how can I trust you?'

You now have two options. One is to go big on reassurance. 'I'd never lie to you, Paulie.' You could say that, particularly if his name is Paulie. The other is to leave him and find someone who isn't rubbish on quite such a regular basis. Which might be wise because frankly you're sick of telling him how great he is when he's not. It's tiring; no matter how often he lends you his Fenwick store card. Anyway, he never tells you how great *you* are. And you *are* great. Of course you are. No, I mean it.

LIE # 79

Laughing at unfunny jokes

Convention dictates that all too often we must push through the pain barrier for reasons of social grace. This may be anything from forcing down inedible food to making small talk with people we would rather shove off a cliff.

High up on this list is laughing at unfunny jokes. 'Ha ha,' you say, clutching your sides, while a not inconsiderable part of you dies. In the end you may grow so used to pretending to chuckle you lose track of what's funny. This can lead to serious behavioural problems, culminating in you chuckling along to videos of cats on YouTube.

There is a pecking order at work here. Who is recounting the tale? If it's a younger sibling or lowly work colleague there's no need to simulate a snicker, just tell them to shove off. If on the other hand, the teller is your boss/ your host/your spouse/the Queen/Kanye West, then it is your duty to laugh, wipe your eyes and declare: 'My word, what a funny joke that was, without question.' This statement underlines the quality of the gag and leaves the joker in no doubt as to your belief in its power.

You meet someone at a party. They are attractive, have big eyes and lickable skin. You like them.

'I know a good joke!' they say.

'Great!' you reply. 'I love good jokes! I probably love you too!'

'What did one tomato say to the other tomato?'

'I don't know!'

'Banana!'

'Ah-ha-ha-ha-ha-ha you are so funny shall we go upstairs now?'

You are at a job interview. It's a job you really want (head of security for Batman and Robin). The interviewer makes a joke about Batman not really being a superhero and Robin being weedy.

'Ha, that's really funny,' you say, even though you are a massive fan of both superheroes and thus highly affronted.

Stop. Why are you doing this? There's really no need. Why not try standing your ground for a change? You don't have to laugh if it's not funny, and certainly not if it offends. This is known as 'integrity' – a word or concept with which you might not be familiar.

Here's an example. You are round at your boss's house having dinner. He tells a joke about prostitutes. The punchline is demeaning to both women and carrots. Instead of laughing you draw attention to this. On Monday he calls you into his office.

'You were right not to laugh at my joke on Saturday,' he says. 'Well done. Unfortunately, you are now fired.'

You thank him before playing a recording of Saturday's conversation. You are unsacked, receive a promotion and an extra three weeks' holiday. Proof – if proof were needed – that you don't have to laugh at unfunny jokes.

Another example. The British prime minister attends an exclusive reception in the former Soviet Union. A room full of dignitaries stands around as the premier recounts an amusing tale.

'In my country we have saying,' he says, two-litre bottle of vodka in hand. 'Why have cow when you have woman!'

'That's not funny at all,' says the PM. 'Is it supposed to be a joke?'

'Oh dear,' replies the president, 'and now we invade your stinky country.'

A sixteen-year intractable war between these two nations ensues, until eventually a truce is declared. Well done, prime minister, for sticking to your guns!

So you see, you don't have to laugh if you don't find something funny. You're better than that. Unless we're talking about this particular entry in the book. Come on, surely it deserves more than that?

LIE # 80

"The dog ate my homework."

This is a classic in the 'haven't done my homework' litany. It's such a classic it's become a cliché. Its use can only be condoned in two circumstances.

Firstly, if it's the truth, the dog really did eat your homework. This would be extraordinary, unless your homework was say, make a model of the Tower of London from beef. Even if that did happen you might be better off thinking of a different excuse.

Secondly, the double bluff. Saying that the dog ate your homework is obviously such a clichéd lie that maybe it's true. Maybe the dog really did eat your homework, thinks the teacher, because only someone whose dog really had eaten their homework would use that as an excuse.

But really, because it's such a cliché, 'the dog ate my homework' is not a very good excuse for not doing your homework. Though the principle behind it – that if you are going to lie to get away with something (in this case homework) make the lie so wacky and out there that it must be true – is a good one.

(This is along the same lines as the Obvious Wig

264

Gambit. This is where a man wears a wig that looks so *obviously* like a wig that you think it must be his real hair, because no one would wear a wig like that. It's risky but mind-bending.)

So variants of the 'the dog ate my homework' lie are: that your dad has wallpapered it to the wall; that it has been exploded because someone thought it was a bomb; or that it has been taken away by an extra-terrestrial life form to inform people on another planet as to what life is like on Earth.

Sometimes, if it's really important homework that you've not done, and you really will be in trouble, you have to go nuclear. You have to play the death card. 'Sorry, I haven't done my maths homework. I tried to do it, but I couldn't see the sums through my tears because *my mother has died*.'

This really does put a full stop to that conversation, and you won't be asked for the maths homework in question. But it will be undermined when your mum turns up for parent–teacher evening.

One of the boldest excuses for not doing your homework, and this really has to be used carefully by a real expert, is the non-lie.

It goes like this:

Teacher: Where's your homework?
You: Look . . . the truth is . . . I was going to make up some lie or something about the dog eating it, but I thought my teacher is too smart to be taken in by that. So I'm not going to lie to you – I simply haven't done it.

265

It's a high-risk strategy. But if you can pull it off – and it requires careful reading of your teacher – then it can work wonders. It simultaneously marks you out as an honest person, while praising your teacher as a smart person, when we all know that neither of those things are true.

But all these excuses are becoming antiquated because much of the homework in today's schools is done on computers and submitted by uploading it to a school computer. So these days the best excuse might be: 'The dog ate my USB stick.'

And that almost sounds believable.

When you were at school, did any of you ever tell the classic lie, 'The dog ate my homework'?

Lee:

I used to say my mum ate my homework, because they knew my mum was crazy and so they used to believe me. You get far less hassle if you say your mum's eaten your homework.

David:

No teacher wants to deal with that one.

Lee:

They'd just say to each other, I've met his mum and she probably did, so just leave it.

Did you tell any other lies at school?

Lee:

Oh, I told loads. I tried everything you could think of. The most elaborate thing I did was during an English lesson. I was basically messing around and being really disruptive so my teacher reported me to my head of year and sent me to see him in his office. I was absolutely terrified, so do you know what I did? I got a compass – is that what they were called, those things you used to draw a circle?

David:

A *pair* of compasses. I don't know why, but those things with a spike that you used to draw a circle were called a pair of compasses.

Lee:

Like a pair of trousers.

David:

Yes, but with the word compasses instead of trousers.

Lee:

Right, well I got one of those and I ever so gently nicked my face, just gently, just tiny little nick, nick, nicks so that a little bit of blood came out, then I smeared it all over my face, got some gravel, pushed that into the blood and then I literally walked in his office and went, 'Hi, you wanted to see me?' And he went. 'Now listen . . . er, what have you done to your face?' And I said, 'Oh I was just running to get here as fast as I could and I just fell over and bashed my face. I've literally just done it.' And he went, 'Well. Listen . . .' and then he just gave up. He was looking at me and I could tell he was thinking, damn, he's just had a really serious injury, so he let me go. It completely diffused the whole situation.

David:

I've never been in a room before when a diagnosis of sociopathy has actually come through.

David, did you ever make up any excuses for not doing your homework?

David:

No, I was a complete swat, and I believed on a deep level that if I didn't do what they told me to do completely, I would in every way be found out and my punishment would be unimaginably awful. So if they said 'do this', I just did it, and I didn't question it at all. I don't think I developed the part of my brain that could see authority as just some other people trying to make me do a thing until I was about nineteen.

Rob:

And then things really kicked off, didn't they!

Lee:

We used to own the pub next to the school – this was in the seventies – so the teachers would all come in for lunch and get drunk before the afternoon lessons. So there was a certain power shift that was good for me. I was always able to give the teachers my 'don't make my mum spit in your chicken pie' look. I never said it out loud, but I could do it with a look.

LIE # 81

The act of not responding to emails

Not replying to an email isn't a lie, per se, but it is a particularly modern form of dishonesty. The sender is invariably plunged into a state of high anxiety or madness, stricken by the idea that the recipient is dead (never) or avoiding them (always). Let's consider an example.

Man takes woman to dinner. Man and woman pass pleasant evening. Friendly emails are exchanged. Man and woman dine again. Further enjoyment is experienced, plus some fondling. Woman emails man. Man doesn't reply. Woman texts man. Man doesn't reply. Woman drinks entire bottle of vodka.

'Perhaps he's dead!' she says to a friend, sobbing.

'He's not dead, he's ghosting.'

'Ghosting?'

'Ghosting. The act of disappearing without notice in order to avoid any social awks.'

'What a git.'

'Word.'

Modern forms of communication have enabled this insidious form of cowardice to creep into our behaviour.

The silent partner thinks: *I'm not that into this person but rather than tell them I'll simply recede. That will be much easier for me and that's all I care about.* The other party on the other hand is rendered confused, desperate and reduced to asking strangers what they think's happened to you. Another example.

Man emails person about job. Person doesn't reply. Man is uncertain whether person received email. Man re-emails ('Just checking whether you received my email.'). Person doesn't reply. Man emails again ('Some clarification would be very helpful going forward.'). Person doesn't reply. Man emails a fourth time ('I'M GOING MAD HERE! SAY SOMETHING!'). Person doesn't reply. Man smashes computer keyboard, throws self out of window (luckily lives in a bungalow).

Social scientists have traced this inability to 'man up' to the end of national service in 1963. This seems to be the point at which the 'backbone' went out of Britain. 'People have lacked balls ever since,' says John, a leading social scientist. 'However, it's the advent of the mobile phone which has truly crystallised our behaviour into the silent spinelessness and lack of courtesy many of us now experience on a daily basis.'

One final example. Woman emails friend. 'Hey, hun, you want to come to my thing Friday?' Friend doesn't respond, considers all options for that evening. Woman waits dignified amount of time (a day), emails again: 'Me again, sorry but need to know numbers x.' Friend doesn't reply, now has three options tabled for Friday but wants to see if better offer comes through. Woman waits a dignified amount of time (ninety-seven minutes): 'Need answer either way tomorrow latest.' Friend doesn't reply. Woman punches wardrobe, complains to everyone in social circle. Woman emails next day: 'You OK? Take it you're not coming?' Woman considers options, decides to go to cocktail bar with richer, more successful friend, emails back: 'Sorry for slow response, hun, been super busy. Would love to be there but unfortch got a clash that night – drinks soon? xx'.

We hope you agree it is time to put an end to the frustrating feebleness that now pervades our society. Just reply STOP to the text we sent. We also sent you an email. In fact we sent it twice. Did you get it? It didn't seem to bounce back so we presume you got it. Unless you're on holiday? Perhaps work's really busy at the moment? Or maybe you're dead. It's hard to tell when you don't reply.

LIE # 82

" It definitely *was* a penalty. "

Football managers are notoriously bright. In fact, the ones that wear suits have been known to knot their own ties. But most prefer to conceal their intellect by sounding thick and speaking in clichés. Nowhere is this more evident than in the post-match interview. Here it's perfectly possible for one man to talk to another for five or ten minutes and for nothing at all to be said. Viewers would be equally illuminated if both men did nothing but blow raspberries at each other, or took it in turns to stare silently at a picture of a dolphin before handing back to the studio. Instead though, season after season, year after year, the interviews continue and the sun creeps closer to the earth.

The penalty lie works like this. If a player from his own team falls over, the manager will say it definitely was a penalty. But if it happens to be a player from the other team, the manager will say it definitely wasn't. Unless of course it definitely was, in which case the manager will say he hasn't seen it yet.

Back in the studio they pointlessly replay the action and offer more partisan platitudes while we at home search for the remote control and some meaning in our lives.

Exercises

1. Try to work out how many times a season this lie is told by Premier League managers.

2. Is this figure greater or smaller than the number of times Alan Shearer has seen Phil Collins in concert? Show your working.

3. Imagine that you are a Premier League football manager. Your team is playing on a cold Monday night at St Mary's. One of your players attacks the referee with a corner flag. Do you:

a. Acknowledge the incident and fine your player a month's wages.

b. Insist that it didn't happen and demand that the referee be sacked for being drunk in charge of a football match.

c. Explain that you missed the incident while fiddling with the zipper of your stylish puffer jacket.

LIE # 83

"You'll like it when you get there."

This is a lie commonly told to children who have raised an objection to the destination of an outing. They may well be saying things along the lines of 'I don't want to go' or 'Do I have to go?' or even the definitive 'I'm not going to go'.

This negativity is countered by parents with the words: 'You'll like it when you get there.' This is a lie; the parents say it knowing it to be false. They know their child will not 'like it when they get there' because they are on their way to something that no child (and many adults) could ever like.

Do they really think that their child is going to enjoy a golf club dinner when they get there? Are they going to get caught up in the excitement of Aldi when they arrive? Are they going to actually have a great time at your aunt's funeral – once they've got there?

And in this way parents introduce children to lying at an early age. No wonder children fear becoming grown-ups – with all its deceit and lies and subterfuge.

Never mind, they'll like it when they get there.

275

Exercise

1. Go somewhere you know you won't like when you get there. Do you like it when you get there?

LIE # 84

"Sorry, I'd love to stop, but I'm in a hurry."

So there you are, walking down the street, without, as they say, a care in the world.

It's a lovely day; things are going to be just fine. You've got someone who loves you; you have somewhere to be at no particular time; you've got some money in your pocket and a song in your heart. The last of these being a poetical expression to denote a positive mood – you haven't had an iPod mini stitched into a body cavity like some kind of musical pacemaker.

Then you spot, a few dangerous metres ahead of you, someone nobody wants to talk to, but who wants to talk to you. Worse than a former colleague whose name you can't remember ('Dave? Dan? Jan?'). Worse than an ex and their new squeeze buying throws for the sofa (your sofa, actually, but you're over that). Worse even than the bloke who wants to talk at length about your last gas bill ('How many thermal units did you use last month?').

It's a chugger. A charity mugger.

You can tell because he has a clipboard and seems happy about that.

You only have a few split seconds to evaluate the situation. You're like a jet-fighter pilot suddenly swinging in front of a new target. Is it hostile? Friendly? You've got just micro-moments to decide whether to press the trigger or not. Maybe just shoot anyway, and let the politicians take the flak. You get enough flak as a fighter pilot.

Anyhoo, back to the pavement and back to your current, actual quandary.

What 'good cause' is this guy collecting for? What is it? Bad cancer? Sick kids? Almost dead people in other countries? He's got a sort of blue and red and white tracksuit thing on – what is that? Mencap? People with no food? People with no feet? What disease is blue and red and white? Is it catching? Could this guy have caught it?

He's got his hand stretched out. He's a hand-shaker. He wants to shake your hand. What if he's caught whatever he's collecting money for – Ebola? – by shaking hands with people? Maybe it's a charity for people who have caught things by shaking hands?

Can you snub his handshake?

You don't want to look like you're a handshake snubber.

He might take it personally. He might think you don't like *him*. Not whatever illness it is he's selling. Collecting for.

You shake his hand.

You now have swine flu.

Probably.

It was a trick. They're full of tricks these people.

He's looking you in the eye. He's saying something to you. He's saying how he wants to talk to you about an illness or a plight or a need or a difficulty or something.

Now you're a good person, you know the world needs sorting out. You're better than most. You care. You buy a poppy most Novembers (but if it falls out of your button-hole before the eleventh, you try and seek out a free replacement in gutters at bus stops – after all, you've paid your money, you've paid your respects). Why is he making you feel like you're bad?

And you know this guy's cause will be a good one. It'll be something that needs doing. Like keeping people alive, or making sure dead people don't come back to life. And you know that this is the best way of giving money to charity – signing up so they can claim the Gift Aid and get more money. But do they have to stop people in the street for it?

But then it's not like this guy is doing this for the benefit of his health. Or other people's. He's being paid. Why doesn't he just give his pay to the charity, then go home?

But you don't really feel like asking all these questions now, so you look beyond the man's head. As if there is something behind him that needs your attention. And without any good excuse for not helping him, the world and people in general, you tell the lie that every single person he has looked in the eye that day has already told him:

'Sorry, I'd love to stop, but I'm in a hurry.'

And then you're gone. Hurrying along to nowhere in particular, your eyes scanning the horizon for any more of his kind.

Do you ever lie to charity collectors in the street, or make up excuses for why you can't stop and talk to them?

Lee:
I'm still out of date because I usually go, 'Sorry, I haven't got any change', and they go: 'It doesn't work like that.'

David:
Yeah, they're looking for you to sign up for a direct debit.

Lee:
But you see, I'm such a generous person that there's not a charity that I pass where I don't go I'm actually already signed up. Well, that's not *always* true, but if they say something like we're trying to save the owl, I'll go I'm already signed up, but it turns out I'm trying to save the seagull or something.

David:
There's an owl and a seagull and they're both under house arrest and they're going to kill one. So you say, I'm going to pledge for the owl. That's what I want: I want to kill the seagull!

Rob:
The execution will be at midnight, which is tough on the owl because he'll be wide awake.

David:

Seagulls, they'll take an ice cream off a two-year-old. Seagulls are evil.

Lee:

At least the owl can turn his head away when he's shot. He won't need a blindfold – he can just look the other way.

Rob:

I don't think I've ever refused any sort of charity.

David:

Me neither, if it's for a charity I'll do it for 98 per cent of my normal fee.

Rob:

If it's someone coming to my door, or somebody approaching me in the street, I've always got time to stop and to listen to what the charity's about, but that almost doesn't matter, it's the very act of giving I enjoy and I'm grateful for being given the chance to give. In fact I have a little card that has my account number and my sort code and my mother's maiden name on it, and I hand that over and I say *you* choose a sum, *you* decide what you think I can afford and I'll look forward to supporting the cause. I'm happy to give, that's my motto in life.

Lee:

And my motto, as you know, is: 'I haven't got any change.'

LIE # 85

"She's like a sister to me."

Her? How can you be jealous of *her?* There's no reason at all to be. There's nothing suspicious about our relationship. She's like a sister to me.

For a start, she's not my type at all, is she? I mean, you know I like brunettes – and she's like a blonde who has dyed her hair brunette. I guess some people might think she's attractive. But then some people probably find my sister attractive. Not me.

Yes, I give her a hug sometimes. A nice long hug. But that's just purely platonic. She's been going through quite a hard time with her break-up from her boyfriend. It's just a friendly squeeze. She's like a sister to me.

And yes, she does text a lot. At night. But I'm just being supportive. I just want her to know that she has someone she can call on. Anytime she likes. She's like a sister to me. She did Snapchat me a picture of her legs last week. But that was just a joke. You know, the sort of joke a sister would make.

So, I said I would take her on holiday. To the Pyrenees. Or scuba diving. Or the Trans-Siberian Railway. Or somewhere else that's not really your thing. You wouldn't enjoy it. Yes, we'll be sharing a room, cabin, yurt or whatever there is. It would cost loads to get two rooms. But don't worry, *nothing is going to happen.* How could it? It would be like being in a bed with my sister. I expect we'll just fall straight to sleep. After a goodnight hug.

Yes, I probably will see her in a bikini. We will be on holiday. Has she got a nice body? I hadn't noticed. I don't look at her that way. I mean, I look at her. I have to look at her to see where she is; otherwise I might not be near her when I speak to her. But I wouldn't know if – as you say – she has a good body. It would be like ogling my sister.

I wish you two could get along a bit better. I think you would like her if you gave her a chance. We just get on. Is that a crime? Yes, you might have caught me looking at her photos on Facebook, but I just wanted to click 'like' on them so she'd know I liked them. She has some really fun-looking friends.

Yes, OK. We did kiss one time. But that was ages ago. Before I met you, I think. We were both drunk. But yes, we did kiss. For quite a while. With tongues. But it didn't mean anything. She's like a sister to me.

So please, don't worry.

86

The art gallery lie
(Or: the inability to say what you really think of a picture for fear of sounding like a fool)

So you're on a date. And instead of going to the cinema, or the pub, you've gone on a date to an art gallery. And to make matters worse this was your suggestion. You wanted to make yourself look a bit cleverer than you are. And seeming a bit cleverer than you are is one small step on the path to seeing your date's bum in the moonlight.

Your date seems like they might be clever. They wear glasses, and the first time you met up you arrived to find them reading a book rather than looking at their phone.

You'd prefer to be in a pub, but this is an afternoon date, and you're not sure how they'd feel about you getting blindly drunk in the afternoon. You thought about the cinema, but then you'd have to be quiet and not say any of your famous jokes.

So an art gallery seemed like a really good idea. But you've come to an art gallery that has made things difficult. Because your date picked the gallery and they've chosen one where it isn't clear whether the art inside it is any good or not, because you've never heard of any of the artists it is currently exhibiting. And now you have to judge for yourself the quality of the work inside.

If it had the name of a big famous artist on the sign outside, a dead one, you would know whether it was good or bad. If it said Picasso, or Matisse, or Hockney, or even Gerhard Richter (because you watch the odd bit of BBC Four) then you would know what to think. You would think it was good.

But this art gallery is full of unknown artists. New artists. You've never heard of them. How are you meant to know whether they are any good or not? You keep looking at the labels before the paintings, desperate for a name you might have heard of. But no dice.

You've wandered through the gallery trying to avoid staring at a painting at the same time as your date, but that game has suddenly come to an awkward end. While staring at a particularly uninteresting picture, trying to look like you are on critical fire, your date has moved in next to you, also staring at the work in question. You have both been staring silently at it for some minutes. Only one of you daring to voice a critical conclusion will break the concentration.

What are you going to say about it?

What do you actually think about it? You think it's boring. Abstract. Meaningless. Pointless. A waste of good wall.

But what if it isn't? What if it's a work of genius? A brief, unfettered glimpse into the human condition that wryly references Botticelli, Karl Jung and Tex Avery.

286

And whether it's one thing or another, what will your date think of it? It's key that you must think the same as them if this relationship is going to work. Heaven forbid you should have a different take on it, not at this early stage of getting together.

(In years to come you can disagree on almost everything – from having children to putting brown sauce on chips – but for now you must agree.)

What can you say about it that will hedge your bets, but still sound erudite, witty, informed and most importantly, in agreement with your date?

You need to think of something fairly soon, because you have now been staring silently at this particular work for some minutes, a fact that might suggest you find something truly significant in it.

What to say?

'It's really big, isn't it?' No, makes you sound like an idiot.

'I love it. I'm going to buy it. Whatever the cost.' What if the date hates it? What if it's like £500 million?

'I wouldn't want it in my living room.' Sounds negative, philistine.

'A child could have done that.' Ditto.

'What is it?' No.

If you're staring at it this long, then the date is going to be expecting something more akin to an essay than an off-the-cuff comment.

You need to get your thoughts in order. You must

quickly become an expert on modern art. You try to look at the little label next to the picture in case it's got some starting points, but it's hard because you know you must just keep staring at the work. It will probably just say 'made of paint' or something.

Should you say the truth? That you hate it. You don't understand it. You don't ever want to look at it again. Especially now that it's burned into your retina more powerfully than an eclipse.

You decide upon a tactic that means, although you speak first, they will hopefully provide a key bit of critical information before you do, under the ruse that you are carefully refining your thoughts.

'It's really . . . like . . .'

But the date doesn't jump in.

'It's so . . .'

Still nothing.

'You know, so . . .'

Still nothing.

And then, like an idiot, you say the only words that come to mind: 'It's very yellow, isn't it?'

The date turns away without saying anything.

You've blown it. They think you're a moron. An art moron. No one in glasses likes an art moron. That much you know. You've blown your chances of seeing their bum in the moonlight.

Then you notice – they're wearing an audio-guide headset.

Phew, that was close. You can say what you like – they can't hear a word.

The bum is still in play.

LIE # 87

"I don't know."

Who is that woman next to you in that photo on Facebook?
I don't know.

Where has all the money gone?
I don't know.

Who was that on the phone?
I don't know.

Why is there no food left in the cupboard?
I don't know.

Why were you back so late last night?
I don't know.

Why is the computer's internet history totally blank?
I don't know.

Where is that report I asked you to do?
I don't know.

Who drank all my wine?
I don't know.

Why is there a man in the bedroom?
I don't know.

How did the boss find out I was throwing a sickie?
I don't know.

Why is there porridge all over the sofa?
I don't know.

What is this receipt for?
I don't know.

Why don't you know?
I don't know. Look, I don't know, so there's nothing more we can say about it.

Sometimes a question comes along, out of the blue, that you need a really good answer for. But sometimes you're so flummoxed by being asked that question that you can't think of a really good truthful answer to it that won't cause a lot of bother.

Under pressure of scrutiny, and without much time to think, it is sometimes useful to fall back on the old favourite: 'I don't know.'

It's quick, it's very hard to prove otherwise, and, used with aplomb, it can provide valuable thinking time for a follow-up lie that builds and expands upon 'I don't know'. The reason you don't know, for example. Or, for the expert dissembler: 'I was going to ask you the same question.' Yeah, see if they know why your trousers are so dirty.

It's a lie because you do know why or how the events in question happened, but the answer, as they say, may tend to incriminate you.

Of course, there are some cases where the answer 'I don't know' seems a little implausible. Like 'Why did you miss my birthday party?' or 'Why did you invade Iraq?' But you can generally breeze through that.

In the right hands, you don't need any other lie than 'I don't know'. But be warned, using it too frequently could give the impression that you are an idiot. Use it only when under extreme duress.

LIE # **88**

66 I think I would get on really well with Richard Osman* 99 if we ever met.

I think I would get along really well with Richard Osman, if we ever met. I think we would have quite an interesting chat, if only we could ever get in the same room as each other. I mean, I think we're quite similar. We like similar things. I like all the things that he is interested in, which means that he would be interested in all the things I am interested in, because they are the same things that he is interested in. Things like facts and things to do with his show, which I love. And he must love too because he does it.

And we would both have a laugh too, if we ever met. Because we both share a similar sense of humour. Because I laugh at all his jokes already, when I see him on TV, and I think he would laugh at all mine too. Because they are sort of similar to his. Not so much jokes like Jimmy Carr does (I think I would get on well with him too) but more

* Or Ricky Gervais, Richard Hammond, Bryan Ferry, David Gower, Rhod Gilbert, Morrissey, Tim Brooke-Taylor, Gordon Ramsey, Viscount Linley, Gary Lineker, Ant and/or Dec, Matt LeBlanc, David Dimbleby, Martin Clunes, Phillip Schofield, Alan Hansen, Nick Knowles (anyone famous basically).

like funny thoughts. Which he thinks of off the top of his head. I can think of things off the top of my head too, so I think he would like that.

The trouble is, despite the fact that we would have a lot to talk about and a lot to laugh about if we ever did meet, we have not yet met. I put this down to a number of factors.

First, we move in different circles. Richard spends most of his time presenting his quiz shows, so spends his time, I guess, in the studio, or making up questions in an office. Whereas I, well, don't. I have my job at the bookmakers, which is all very well, but it does mean that I don't cross paths with Richard, and although I keep my eyes peeled for him, I don't think he is a regular at my bookies. He may not visit Great Yarmouth at all. I imagine he may well like a bet but – like me – probably finds it more convenient to do it online. I can't say I blame him.

Knowing how busy he is, and how unlikely it is that we will cross paths unless one of us takes the initiative, I have been trying to make a meeting happen between us – safe in the knowledge that when we do meet we will have plenty to talk about and become very close friends.

He seems so nice, someone I could easily introduce friends and family to without it being awkward or embarrassing. Oh hi, meet my friend Richard Osman. That's right, Richard Osman from teatime smash-hit TV shows *Pointless* and *Celebrity Pointless*.

But before that is going to happen, one of us is going to have to get their act together and be the bigger man

(in moral terms I mean, no one is bigger than Richard in actual size – he is *so* tall!) and make it so that we finally meet up. And it's probably going to have to be me.

It goes without saying that a great way of meeting him would be to appear on one of his shows. Either *Pointless* or *Celebrity Pointless* or his latest show, *Two Tribes*, which is just him on his own and is just brilliant. Going on *Two Tribes* would be great because he's the only host, so there's no chance that I would get stuck talking to Alexander Armstrong (who is OK) while Richard and me could be having a *great laugh*.

So, I have applied for *Pointless* seven times; *Two Tribes*, sixteen times; and *Celebrity Pointless*, five times. I got picked for an audition for *Pointless*. An audition? Who knew they had auditions for quiz shows? Me and Donald from the shop went down to London; we were really looking forward to it. But much to my great surprise you don't actually get to meet Richard, or the other one, at the auditions. I mean, if they're not at the auditions, how are they going to know if they're going to have chemistry with you? It doesn't make any sense to me. Instead you just meet loads of 'producers' who don't know anything about great banter.

And do you know what they said, these producers, they said that they really enjoyed my audition, and thanks for doing it, but they wouldn't be proceeding any more with my application for the show. Can you believe it? I thought maybe it was Donald so I have applied since then with different people, and under different names, but to no avail.

Who are these so-called 'producers' that they think they know better than me as to who would get on well with Richard? They are simply trying to keep him for themselves.

There are other ways of getting in touch. I have tried tweeting him a couple of times an hour – just banter about the state of the UK today and footie – but he never gets back to me. Well, he must have so many people tweeting him he can't respond to them all. And he obviously blocks people he doesn't know.

And I have tried being in the audience for *Two Tribes*. I shouted him a few 'bon mots' before being asked to leave by the security people. After the sixth time I was told that I am banned from all recordings of all TV shows involving Richard Osman. This does seem a bit heavy-handed, but then there are some nutcases out there. I don't blame them, they don't know how well Richard and I would get on if only we could meet.

So now I just have to wait to get a glimpse of him as he gets in his car at the end of the night. I have to shout to make my voice heard over the mob. 'Richard! Richard! I've made you a picture out of milk bottle tops and some of my hair! Come on, Richard, give us a smile!' Just banter – trying to make him look my way, trying to make a connection.

Because I *know* that me and Richard Osman would really get on well, if only we could ever meet.

LIE # 89

" *I'm going to leave my wife.* "

You've been meeting the same man every Tuesday afternoon for seven years in a hotel in Stevenage.

'You really understand me,' he says, zipping up his fly.
'Thanks,' you say, popping your skirt back on. 'Are you going to leave your wife?'
'Definitely,' he replies. 'Just need to sort out a few things. Admin mainly. See you next Tuesday.'

The man has no plans to leave his wife. Alternatively, he may have every intention. But it's not going to happen. They've been married eleven years. Their histories are intertwined. They can't remember which of them bought *The Best of Bob Dylan: Volume 8* or *The Blair Years* by Alastair Campbell. Plus they have thirteen children, which could be a complicating factor.

But where there's life there's hope.

'He says he's going to ditch her and we're moving to Anglesey!' you tell Diane over a Wolf Blass.
'He's been saying that since you met him,' says Diane, filling in the crossword.
'Yes, but this time it was different.'

'In what way?'
'He said it in German.'

Whenever he thinks you might stop offering up your services he reiterates his intention to leave his wife. He would, however, baulk at the notion that he's just in it for the thrill and the broken biscuits (you work at a biscuit factory). Clearly, he cares about you. Why else would he lavish you with gifts (lingerie, nurses uniforms, blind-folds)?

'I love him,' you say.
   'Three across – "clearly presented" – five letters.'
   'I've met his wife you know. She's a slag.'
   'You're the slag!'
   'How dare you. Try "lucid".'

The spark has gone from his marriage, replaced by a glow barely visible to the naked eye. Things used to be special, including interesting positions and breakfast in bed. Not now though. There's no question they're growing apart – him with his sunflowers, her with her interest in extreme male bodybuilding. But he's never going to leave her.

'Classic man,' says Diane, filling in the letters. 'Ain't going nowhere. Gutless. Classic man. Six letters, "brief in speech".'
   'Look at my legs!' you declare. 'Don't these legs deserve something more than forty-seven minutes a week? I'm still a beautiful woman! Does "terse" fit?'

The following Tuesday you meet the man in the usual place.

'You're not going to leave your wife are you?' you say.

'Course,' he replies. 'Just got a few bits and pieces to sort out. I bought you these nipple tassels.'

'Thanks,' you reply. 'But you're not, are you?'

'Not what?' he says, lifting his loosened tie over his head.

'Going to leave your wife. I know you're not. Perhaps we should stop pretending that you are.'

'You like pretending, don't you?' he says, lustily.

'I'm serious,' you say. 'In fact I think we should stop doing this. There's no point. It's over.'

The man stops in his tracks. A solitary tear rolls down one cheek. He wipes it away before looping his tie back over his head.

'What about the biscuits?' he says.

90

66 The wine's great, thanks. 99

'Would you like to try the wine, sir?'

Not really, you think. You have no idea what it is you're tasting it for. But the waiter is asking, he seems keen for you to have a try, holding the bottle in front of you with the suggestion that he might be trying to defraud you somehow – can you spot if this is a genuine wine label or a fake?

It's not like you try the wine when you're having a bottle at home. You don't pour yourself a quarter of an inch into a glass and then mull it around in your mouth before pronouncing it 'great, thanks' and pouring out some more.

But you're in a restaurant, and *she's* watching your every move. So you say: 'Yes, I'd love to try the wine, thanks.'

The waiter knows. He knows you're a fraud. He knows you have no idea what it is you are tasting it for. He knows, not because of some slip on your part, but because it's true of everyone.

What is it you're meant to be tasting it for? I mean, are you meant to be checking that there's actually wine in

the bottle? That the wine hasn't somehow been substituted for some other liquid – cranberry juice, Bovril, horse blood? Is it some kind of vast European wine fraud that you alone are in charge of checking? But surely the fraudsters would have done something to cover their tracks in this case? They would at least have made their pretend wine taste a bit like wine. Enough for you to think it's wine anyway.

So the waiter pours a little bit and you knock it back into your open mouth like you've seen other people do.

You slosh it around a bit like mouthwash, like you've seen other people do.

It doesn't taste of blood or paint or washing-up liquid. It doesn't taste amazing. But then it was the second cheapest wine. (Not the cheapest, *she* mustn't think you are a skinflint. Women don't like skinflints. But equally you're not made of money. Why can't being sensible with money appear sexy to women?)

It tastes – gun to your head – like . . . wine. Red wine. Which is good, because it *is* red wine.

But what are you meant to be tasting it *for*? In the back of your head something about 'cork rot' floats in. Are you meant to be tasting it for cork rot? What is cork rot? What does it taste like? If it tastes like wine then you really are in trouble?

But this wine bottle's got a screw top? Can it have cork rot with a screw top? Doubtful. Is there such a thing as screw-top rot? Maybe? What does it taste like?

You've been sloshing it around for a long time now. Are you meant to spit it out? You've seen people spit it out. In films about wine and TV programmes with Oz Clarke. And in a cartoon in *Private Eye*.

Are you meant to be thinking of words to describe it? What comes to mind?

'Wine-y . . . with a hint of . . . cheap wine . . .'

Now that you really concentrate, with *her* and *him* staring you full in the face, it does taste slightly of dung. Just as it catches the back of your epiglottis. Is that a good thing? Is a Merlot mean to taste a bit dung-y? Or is that a bad thing? Is that what screw-cap rot tastes of? Is that dung flavour a mark of excellence, or is it exactly the sort of thing you're meant to point out when you send the wine back? Or is a dung-y flavour something you just have to live with when you're ordering the second cheapest wine on the list? To avoid a dung-y flavour, should you have gone with the third cheapest? Or even the fourth? A whole £1.50 more?

Do they deliberately make the second-cheapest wine taste of dung to trip up skinflints like you? Would the cheapest wine taste even more of dung?

It's been in your mouth a long time now, sloshing around. It's almost like you're using your mouth as a tiny washing machine. You become acutely aware of your tongue. It seems enormous. And pointless. What is it doing there? In the middle of your mouth?

Should you mention the dung flavour? It's only a bit

dung-y. It's maybe just that it's been in your mouth so long. Need to get rid of it. Sort of getting more dung-y the more you slosh it around. You're directing it into parts of your mouth even your dentist doesn't know about. Behind the teeth, under the tongue, almost through your nose.

Need to get rid of it. But as soon as you knock it back you're going to have to say something.

Gulp.

'The wine's great, thanks.'

He pours *her* a glass.

She puts it to her lips – her beautiful lips – and takes a sip. Then she gives you a smile fixed somewhere between politeness and pain, like somebody not really enjoying a glass of dung-y flavoured wine. Your chink your glass to hers, and neck another mouthful. Next time, if there ever is a next time, you'll pay the extra £1.50.

When you're in a restaurant and a wine waiter brings over a bottle and pours some out for you to taste, do any of you know what you're actually tasting for?

Rob:

Well, I learned this when I did the BAFTA-nominated programme, *The Trip*. You may have seen it, it was BAFTA-nominated. All you're meant to do in that situation is check it's not corked; it's as simple as that. You're not meant to go, 'Oh that's lovely, very nice.' All you're meant to say is: 'Yep, it's not corked, that's fine.'

And is that what you do in restaurants now?

Rob:

I did for a while, after *The Trip*, but now I've gone back to: 'Oh that's lovely, have you got any more?' Actually, I was just given a thing for my birthday that's basically a needle that you stick in through the cork and then use to pour out however much wine you want. Then when you take the needle out it's like you've not even opened the bottle.

Lee:

I thought you were going to say you draw out the needle and stick it straight in your vein.

Rob:

Well, once again, you are showing yourself to be a philistine, Lee. It's actually very clever. And if you want to try a wine, but you think I'm not going to finish it, you can try a little bit and it's like you haven't opened it.

Am I the only person that's finishing the bottle?

David:

Er, no, you're not.

❝I can walk along *and* look at my phone.**❞**

It used to be considered *impossible* to walk through busy city streets while looking, not ahead at the pedestrians and traffic in front of you, but down at a small screen six inches away from your face. It was received wisdom, but then they used to think that the sun went round the Earth, and that Noel Edmonds wouldn't get on TV again after *Noel's House Party*.

Ever since the invention of the iPhone, people have felt that there *must* be a way that they could continue to walk down crowded streets and cross busy roads while still texting, surfing the net, flicking through Facebook and generally looking at something other than where they were going. There *had* to be.

Yes, people needed to get to where they were going, but they also needed to carry on looking at their phone and running their finger across it. How could these two seemingly incompatible tasks be combined? The trouble being that if someone tries to do both at once, they end up walking into people, bollards, roads, cars, death, etc.

Would it take some new sort of technology? Would a wholesale reorganisation of the infrastructure of urban areas make it work? For a while it looked like nothing was going to solve the problem. It looked as if people were going to have to either stop to look at their iPhones, or not look at them until they got to where they were going. Both options too nightmarish to contemplate.

And then, suddenly, someone, somewhere – no one knows who – thought this revolutionary thought: 'Even though it is patently impossible to both walk along and look at a phone at the same, I'm going to do it. The moment I get to the top of the station escalator.'

And once they did it, everyone started doing it. Obviously, they kept walking into other people, the roads, buses and things. But those dangers were worth it for the pleasure of getting to grips with Freddie Flintoff's latest tweet, or catching the end of an illegal bootleg of *The Big Bang Theory*, series seven.

Problem solved.

The trouble is, it was a lie. No one can look at two things at once. So everyone just keeps bumping into people.

You're probably reading this on an iPad or Kindle or something as you march down the high street.

You're about to bump into a man coming the other way.

Look up!

Look up!

Stop reading this!

Ouch.

LIE # 92

" Er – hahahahahahahahahaha – yeah – right! "

You're in a nightclub.

The music is *too loud*.

Yet despite the fact that the music is *too loud*, someone is trying to talk to you about *something*.

Why are they talking? To you? You're in the nightclub for a number of reasons:

1. *You want to dance.*
2. *You are drunk and want to drink some more.*
3. *You want to try and get off with someone.*
4. *You are the DJ. Or the DJ's mate. Or the DJ's girlfriend. Or the DJ's mate's girlfriend's mate.*
5. *You have made a dreadful mistake.*

Or all of the above. But definitely not: Because you fancy listening to a long conversation about *something*.

All you know for certain is that the conversation they are trying to have with you is about *something*. The fact is, the music is *too loud*, and as a result you can't really hear what they are talking about. Maybe it's that they saw

a really funny joke in *Nuts* magazine. Maybe they have failed their driving test because they crashed into a horse.

Everyone else seems to have noticed the music is *too loud* for conversation. They're all dancing and drinking and getting off with people and eyeballing the DJ's mate's girlfriend's mate.

But not this person: they're ploughing on talking about *something*. What *is* it about? The snooker? Sine waves? Sad things?

It's too late now to say 'Pardon?' or 'I can't hear you' or 'The music's *too loud*' – they've already been talking for a minute about *something*. What? Trousers? How they're having their bone marrow removed to give to their brother?

Is it something about what you were talking about before? What was that? No, it's gone. It is very late. And the music is *too loud*.

It must be something important, because they're really banging on about it. It might be how they think it's ludicrous that there's a man in the loo who wants a pound for handing over a hand towel. Or it might be that their parents died in a car crash yesterday.

You lean in even closer in the hope of catching something of what they're saying: a word, a syllable, maybe just the tone of their voice. You feel the warm, beery wind of their breath puffing into your ear drum, droplets of their spittle – a heady cocktail of old saliva and Smirnoff Ice – landing on your ear lobe.

But you still can't hear. You pull an expression that you hope is the subset of amused and concerned. A sort of half-smile with a frown. You try a head movement that you think might suggest both 'yes' and 'no'.

Then, just as a quiet track comes on, they stop talking about *something* (Soup? Syria?) and turn to look at you. They want your take on *something* (iPhones? Eye surgery? Maybe they're trying to chat you up. Yes, you.).

And what do you say? Do you say 'I'm sorry I didn't catch a word of that'? No, you lie. They were probably saying something sort of amusing so you mumble something along the lines of: 'Er – hahahahahahahahaha – yeah – right!'

They look at you like you are *absolutely mad* and walk off.

Perhaps they had killed a horse.

LIE # 93

"Merry Christmas!"

Let's be perfectly clear, Christmas is never merry. It's a lot of other things, but never merry. Yet waft away the bum fog of a billion Brussels sprouts and all you can hear is this empty phrase echoing back and forth across the frosted rooftops. Bah humbug! I hear you say, Christmas is a magical time of year. Well you're wrong. It isn't, and here's why.

Christmas now begins in September:
As soon as the tanned hand of summer meets the icy paw of autumn, consumerist Christmas officially begins. Department stores transform whole floors into grottos of novelty tat and magazines demand that we order our commemorative Christmas trinkets early to avoid disappointment. But it's impossible to avoid disappointment. Disappointment is the only legitimate response to the nakedness of corporate Christmas masquerading as tradition. You would feel less disappointment if you retreated to your bed until January with nothing but a ball of string for company and a glass of water for sustenance.

Christmas adverts take over and John Lewis gets seasonally smug:

Commercial breaks get longer and more frequent as we creep closer to Christmas day, and by the time we get to Christmas Eve it can take as long as thirteen hours to watch an ITV screening of *Trading Places*.

In mocked-up Victorian streets famous faces exchange their beaming smiles for stockings of cash, their grins as fake as the snow that falls around them. Look, there's John Bishop grinning by a turkey! And Mary Berry pulling a cracker with Trevor Eve! And isn't that Anton Du Beke on a sledge with some ham? These famous people really are funny and Christmassy!

Of course the most irritating advert of all is whatever John Lewis fling in our mince pies. Firstly, there's the expectation of the general public, who from October onwards like to speculate as to what the ad will be. Then there's the collective outpouring of emotion as people clamour to be the first to admit they shed a tear at the manipulative tale. It's not art and it's not clever, it's just a contemporary pop star singing somebody else's song while someone or something finds love in an unexpected place. Never forget that they are only telling you the story of a hedgehog and his shoebox because they are hoping to sell you some towels. This tends to get overlooked as you hum along to Paolo Nutini singing Coldplay's 'Fix You' or whatever it happens to be.

The office Christmas party:
You go to the office Christmas party and ruin relation-ships with people you have otherwise rubbed along with pretty well. Alcohol loosens both your tongue and your trousers, and you are tossed into the back of a taxi by your horrified boss. He gives the driver twenty quid to take you home, and you your P45 to take to your next employer. You spend the following morning with a head like a smashed lamp, flushing red at the memory of the night before.

Queues in shops go on for miles:
. . . and miles and miles and miles and miles and miles. To try and speed things up most stores hire temporary staff to work on the tills. The trouble is, these temporary staff don't know how anything works, so you stand in line feeling your life disappear as a thirteen-year-old holds a dressing gown above his head and shouts desperately for somebody to tell him how much it costs.

You go home to stay with your parents:
You really like the idea of staying in your own place over Christmas and hanging out with your likeminded friends, but the twin pressures of family and tradition render this idea nothing but a dream. Inevitably, you find yourself back in the awful town or village you grew up in and you feel like a ghost walking through the memories of your own mind. On Christmas Eve you venture to the

local pub and note that the same man who was sat at the fruit machine when you had your first pint, aged fifteen, is still there hoping three lemons will come in. They do, in the shape of old school friends who call you by a long forgotten nickname and shun you for your fancy city ways.

Back home you climb into bed in your old room, only now it doubles as your parents' office, and you feel sad that your big teddy is surrounded by packets of printer paper and a wall planner. The next morning more family arrive, so you are forced to spend the next three nights sleeping on an ironing board under the stairs.

The dreaded Christmas dinner:
Having spent the night on the ironing board under the stairs you arrive at the table for the Christmas meal hunched and nursing a cricked neck. You sister's partner who you openly despise is drunk and flirting with your widowed nan. So far she has spent the holiday snoring in the best armchair with a large-print Agatha Christie on her knee and blowing off. Your mum asks if you would mind sitting squashed up by the table leg in a plastic chair from the garden. You do so, and after about ten minutes, an intense pain in your lower back competes with your stiffening neck for the title of Ache of the Day. Dinner is served and people laugh at your insistence on having something vegetarian. Your mum asks if you can eat pigs in blankets if she cuts them up 'really small', but

you politely decline and tuck in to your pasta and roast potatoes. Crackers are pulled, hats are put on and enough food to block a toilet for the next two weeks is eaten. After the meal, you nip upstairs and smoke a cigarette while leaning out of your bedroom window. Through the darkness, hundreds of tiny orange glows wink back at you from the fags of others just like you.

Somebody dies in the Christmas Day EastEnders:
I could elaborate but it seems unnecessary.

The Queen gives a speech:
I could elaborate but it seems unnecessary.

An *Only Fools and Horses* you have seen a thousand times is shown again:
I could elaborate but it seems unnecessary.

Boxing Day repeats itself:
On Boxing Day the shops are full of people fighting each other to buy things they don't want at reduced prices. Somewhere in the country it has snowed and the news gives cold weather warnings and runs mobile phone footage of skidding cars colliding on a motorway. You watch a report on some stranded hikers who spent Christmas Day in Scotland's most isolated pub, and a man outside Selfridges tells you that high-street profits are up on last year. You flick channels and a different man outside Sel-

fridges tells you that high-street profits are down on last year. You pack your presents into a bag to give to a charity shop and have a snooze during *The Great Escape*.

Cold turkey:
The next few days are a whirlwind of boring conversations with neighbours you assumed were dead and arguments over board games. Without exception, all of your friends seem to have been having a better time than you and you vow to yourself that next year you'll spend Christmas at home. But you won't, and you know it. Next year, you'll be back in the family home, sleeping on the ironing board and picking the meat out of your veggie dinner from the discomfort of the plastic garden chair as if you'd never been away.

Merry Christmas!

Lies to watch out for from . . . **TV chefs**

LIE # 94

66 This meal can be ready
in fifteen minutes. 99

As we ride home through the gloaming, broken by the office, and one day closer to death, our thoughts inevitably turn to food. What can we shove in our stomachs and how quickly can we shove it there? Speed is a crucial part of this equation and the ace card of the takeaway; but its joker is health. So every now and then we have to seek other solutions, and that means home cooking.

TV chefs used to tell us that meals took half an hour, and that sounded about right. Then they started vying for our attention by claiming they had recipes that could be cooked from scratch in twenty-five minutes. Then, just as people started to say, hang on a minute, it takes me ten minutes to peel and chop an onion, they brought the time down even further to fifteen minutes. *Fifteen* minutes? It takes most people that long to wash a pan and find the bottle of balsamic.

Now, we're not saying that it's *impossible* to cook these meals in fifteen minutes. That would be legally foolhardy.

But unless you're a professional chef or have an army of minions preparing the ingredients in advance it seems pretty difficult. As a demonstration of this argument here is a minute-by-minute breakdown of this writer's pathetic attempt to make some sausage tagliatelle.

First up, the recipe instructs me to squeeze the meat of four spicy sausages out of their skins and into a casserole pan. I start my stopwatch.

00:00

I walk to the fridge and root around for the four sausages. There are only three there. Where's the fourth one gone? Has Mark eaten it? I hope not, I still haven't forgiven him for having my yoghurt.

01:00

I phone Mark. It goes to voicemail. I leave a message. 'Hi Mark, it's me. Have you eaten my sausage? Call me as soon as you get this, I'm on a deadline.'

01:30

I hang up and shuffle through the post. Bills, bills, bills, bills, bills. How many times do I have to tell them? Bill doesn't live here any more.

02:30

My phone rings. It's Mark. He sounds like he's underwater, but he says he's on a train. I ask him if he's eaten my sausage. He says he gave it to Claire to stop her crying. I tell him I'm pretty cross as I was looking forward

to making some sausage tagliatelle. The phone cuts out. I hang up.

03:30

I decide to use just three sausages, and as instructed squeeze the meat out of the skins and into the pan. A blob of sausage falls onto the floor. I pick it up and blow the hair off it. I put it in the pan, but can't stop thinking about the hair that was on it. I fish it out of the pan, burning my fingers in the process. I run them under the cold tap. At the sink, I see our neighbour through the kitchen window – she's cooking too. I wave at her with my good hand. She shuts her blinds.

05:00

I look at the recipe. It tells me to add two sprigs of fresh rosemary. 'Sprig' is such a funny word, I think. Who thought of that? I march around the kitchen chanting the word 'sprig' over and over again. After a while it doesn't even sound like a word. 'Sprig, sprig, sprig, sprig, sprig, sprig, sprig.' I wonder if I'm the only person in the whole wide world saying 'sprig' over and over again at this particular moment in time. The possibility makes me tingle with excitement.

08:00

The recipe instructs me to finely chop two rashers of streaky bacon. I do this as best I can but there's something about the texture of the bacon and the way it slides about on the chopping board that makes it quite difficult.

Maybe the knife is a bit blunt. I fish around in the drawer for a better one and find an old key. It looks familiar but I can't think what on earth it opens. Maybe it's for Jen's flat? I wonder what she's up to. Maybe she's chanting the word 'sprig' over and over again in somebody else's kitchen. I turn on Facebook and look at pictures of her. There she is smiling on a boat. I turn off Facebook and go back to the bacon. I tear it up with my fingers and chuck it in the pan.

12:00

I jump about a bit in the recipe to where I can see the word Chianti. I need to add 125 ml of it to the pan with the three sausages in. I open the bottle, take a sniff and pour out what I think must be about 125 ml into a glass. It doesn't look like much. I add some more, but now it looks like loads. I take a sip, and then another. It tastes like life itself. I open up Spotify and put on some music. I love this song, it really takes me back.

3 hours and 45 minutes later

Mark comes into the kitchen and looks at the black bits of sausage in the pan. He turns the music down and we tell each other stupid jokes. He says he tried to buy me a sausage on the way home but everywhere was shut. I tell him to forget about it, what's a sausage between friends? We admit we're both starving, so we get the cornflakes out and have a massive bowl each. They take about fifteen seconds to make and they taste absolutely amazing.

95

❝Oh hello . . . *you!* How nice to see *you* again!**❞**

Who the hell are they?

They are talking to you; they are looking you square in the eye and talking to you. Asking you how you are. They seem to know you really well. How do they know you? How do you know them? They seem to know a lot about you. They know all about your life and your work and your friends. Really detailed stuff that only someone who knew you really well would know. And if they know all of that about you, you should really know all of that about them.

Who the hell are they? Will they give you a clue? A titbit of info that will start a torrent of connections in your mind? No. They're not giving you anything. It's as if they have already sensed that you don't have a clue about them and they're pushing you to say that you can't remember them. What a git. And they're smiling all the way through it! Like they like you.

Do they know that you don't know them? Did they sense that flash of confusion over your face when they first said hello? Why won't they give you a clue? A place, a

person. They keep talking about you; that's no good, they need to mention a detail about themselves.

It's hard work. Your brain is overheating as it tells your memory cell to chug through all the people you've ever met at the same time as telling your face muscles to pull shapes that look like you are really enjoying this chance meeting. Like it's the best thing that ever happened to you, rather than the worst.

You know what's coming next – you are going to have to ask them something about their life. That'll be hard, given that you don't know who they are, but useful in case they mention something that shocks your memory banks into working.

Which bland question will you go for?

'How are things with you?'
'You still up to the same thing?'
'You work around here, do you?'

All boring, but all useful. And none of them reveal your complete ignorance of the person opposite. But then, just as you have picked your question ('So, things all OK in your world?'), they suddenly they mention a name. A shared acquaintance. Like: 'So, have you seen Jeff/Suzy/Romesh/Jane/Clint/Rodrigo/Melanie/Sven/etc. recently?'

That should be useful. That should be a clue. Something to work with. You should now be able to link them together. But all you're thinking is:

Who the hell is Jeff/Suzy/Romesh/Jane/Clint/Rodrigo/Melanie/Sven/etc.?

It's another dead end. Your mind is like the wall of a police team investigating a murder: random faces on a Perspex wall with ribbons attempting to connect crimes.

'Oh, not for a little while.'

Do they know? They know. They know you don't know who they are.

And then you think, maybe they're in the wrong. Maybe they've got you muddled up with someone else. Someone who looks like you. It can happen. Maybe you should just say: 'Look, I think you've got the wrong person.'

But hang on, that can't be right, they know all about you. You've obviously met them before. But maybe you should just admit it – that you can't quite place them; that you're not sure who they are and you have no idea who Jeff/Suzy/Romesh/Jane/Clint/Rodrigo/Melanie/Sven/etc. is. Then this nightmare will be over.

No. That would be suicide. Suppose they're like your boss or someone? You can't let them know your brain is going. Have to style it out.

You try to act friendly.

'So good to see you.'

Still sounds like you don't know who they are, so you add one of those words that sounds like you know who they are and that you have a level of intimacy with them – 'mate', 'love' or the more modern 'dude' or 'buddy' if your tormentor has a beard.

Useful words, those. Actors call everyone 'darling' because they work with so many people that they can't be expected to know them all. Builders call everyone John for the same reason. You work with a lot of people too. Why can't there be a name for all of them too? 'Sam'? That would work.

Hang on – you haven't been listening to what they've been saying. Did they say something that sounded like a clue? You've missed it now.

If only you had Google glasses on – those special spectacles with a camera linked to the internet – then you'd be able to identify them no problem. You could just whizz through Facebook, link their face to their name and then get the glasses to show you the last picture of a cat they put on their page. Why didn't you get them? Only £1000 – worth every penny to get out of this.

So you keep talking. And they keep talking. Mentioning people, places and things that leave you baffled.

'Anyway,' they eventually say, 'So good to see you again, me, you and Jeff/Suzy/Romesh/Jane/Clint/Rodrigo/Melanie/Sven/etc. should go out for a drink or something soon.'

And you say, yes, that would be great.

And they say, 'OK, see you later mate/love/dude/buddy.'

And then you realise that they can't remember your name either.

And you're both left thinking . . .

Who the hell are they?

324

Do you have a technique for . . . not remembering people's names?

Lee:

A technique for *not* remembering?

David:

Yes, it works brilliantly.

Rob:

I rely on ageing. I find that works very well for me.

David:

Ageing with a bit of not giving a damn about other people.

OK, I could probably have phrased that better. I mean do you have a technique for covering up the fact that you can't remember someone's name?

Lee:

Well, I do the mumble. I do a lot of that. Because most people have got some sort of one-syllable-sounding name, or an abbreviation, you get away with going, 'All right [*mumbles*], how are you doing?'

You just say a noise?

Lee:

Yep. Or you just use the system of remembering their

name in the first place by word association. So, let's say I'd just met someone called Ruth, I might picture her with a roof on her head. The only trouble is, next time I see her, I know I need to picture her with something on her head but I can't remember exactly what it is. So I end up calling her Hattie.

David:

I find the real problem comes when you are at an event like last night [The BAFTAs, where *Would I lie To You?* lost out for the second year running. Have we mentioned that already?] and you might see someone you recognise and you say hello but then you have to introduce them to someone else.

Rob:

Oh, that's awful.

David:

So you end up doing a sort of thing where you say, 'Sorry, have you not met before?' And all you're thinking is please say your names to each other!

Rob:

I'm told that [names a famous old comedian] refers to people as Vice Admiral or Lord Lieutenant or Rear Gunner.

Lee:

Well that's where the phrase 'Luvvie' comes from isn't it. Because nobody knows anyone's name, so they say, 'Hello, Lovey.'

David:

Yes, hello, darling.

Rob:

Yes, but [famous old comedian] will say 'Archbishop, how are you?' so you think, oh he's calling me Archbishop that's nice; he's being ever so familiar with me.

Lee:

Except it turns out it's senile dementia. 'Ah look it's the duke. It's the Duke of Belgium!' When in fact it's just the postman.

96

" *I have seen a ghost.* "

Anybody who claims to have seen a ghost is either:

a. Lying.

b. Mistaken.

c. Trying to get a girl they fancy to join them in their sleeping bag.

So certain am I that ghosts do not exist, I have retired to an attic room at the top of an abandoned orphanage to pen this particular entry. I will write by candlelight and only begin my musings when the clock strikes midnight.

Bong! Bong! Bong! The News at Ten has just started, only two hours to go.

I spy an old trunk in the corner of the attic and tread the creaky boards to take a look inside. Hmm, it's locked. I search a nearby bookcase for the key, but there is none. The wind rattles the shutters and a light patter of rain drums upon the roof. I move to the window and look out across the fields to the church upon the hill. A dark figure stoops behind a gravestone. The air seems thick with a gathering storm.

The church clock strikes midnight, though I swear I counted thirteen chimes. I must be tired. I take the candle from the mantelpiece and pull a chair up to the writing desk. I open my laptop and knock the candle off the desk. The flame catches on one of my discarded travel stockings and burns it away to nothing. I make a note to buy another pair for the return journey. I cannot risk another bout of DVT.

That's strange, I've just had an email with the subject line: 'IS THIS MR JAMES?' Well no, I am not Mr James, whoever he is. And who is this asking, there's no address from the sender? (I don't even know how I got this email; there is absolutely no internet connection here.)

Anyway, where were we? Oh yes, ghosts. Or rather, the lack of them.

Here's a question. In a world where everybody carries a phone camera, and CCTV coverage is so intrusive that someone in a control tower is watching you right now as you pick your nose and flick it across the room, how come nobody has ever captured footage of a ghost? Not one single person.

And here's another question. When somebody says that they used to live in a house that was haunted by the ghosts of twins that were poisoned by their mother who had gone mad after seeing a headless horseman striding about in the woods at dusk, are they a reliable source?

And here's another question. When somebody says that they came down to breakfast one morning to find

that all the plates in the kitchen cupboards had been swapped over, are they a drunk, and had they been out boozing the night before?

Excuse me one moment, I need to stoke the fire. There's a chill in the room and a sudden rush of cool air up the leg of my shorts is troubling my nethers. (I find I write best in shorts, though it raises a few eyebrows from the staff at the British Library.)

There, that's better. Nothing like a flickering fire to occupy the mind. It's funny, the owner of this place, Mr Spook, said that nobody has stayed in this room for over a year, but I've just found a lottery ticket from last week in the grate. Looks like they bought three lines and put number 'six' in each of them. I can't make out the rest of it; it's torn to pieces.

Now where were we? Oh yes, DEATH . . . that's weird, I just typed the word 'Ghost' and it came out as 'DEATH'. That'll teach me to spill Lucozade on my laptop. The keyboard must have gone all funny. Well, it seems to be working now, so I may as well KILL HIM on.

So, here's another question. When somebody says they once picked up a hitch-hiker who climbed in the back seat of their car then disappeared leaving behind a local paper with his picture on the front and a story about the motorbike crash he had been killed in ten years earlier, is that a person you really want as your dentist?

Of course it isn't. Because ghosts don't exist, and any-one who says that they do is an idiot and a liar.

WE CAN SEE YOU

There seems to be a noise coming from the old trunk in the corner of the room. And look, the key was in it all along. How did I miss that last time? I best investigate. Just 'save' this entry first. There we are. Now then, what have we got in here?

Editor's note: This entry for the *Would I Lie To You?* book was delivered by hand to the offices of Faber & Faber wrapped in a burnt travel stocking. The author of the piece is missing.

LIE # 97

"I'm just tired."

You're having a bad time at a party. Everyone has more babies, houses, wedding rings, money and MacBooks than you.

> 'And what do you do?' asks a person you recognise from the telly.
> 'I stuff envelopes from my bedsit.'
> 'Ha!' they say. 'That's so funny. What do you really do?'
> You finish your wine and grab your coat.
> 'I'm going to peel off,' you tell the host.
> 'Not having a good time, hun?' they ask.
> 'Oh no, I am. It's brilliant here. I'm just tired.'
> 'Yes,' they reply. 'You do look terribly tired.'
> 'Thanks,' you say, and exit.

Just like eating, twerking and making illegal downloads, feeling knackered is a universal experience and part of life. Claiming fatigue is therefore the ultimate excuse for anyone who wishes to make a quick getaway. It's the perfect blanket to hide behind, or indeed under.

You're on a blind date. It's not going well. Your date has admitted to spells inside for GBH and is showing little remorse for his crimes.

332

'Would you like to go on for a drink somewhere?' he asks. 'We could even go back to mine, though I warn you the heating's jammed so you'll probably need to take most if not all of your clothes off.'

'That's very kind of you,' you say, 'but I'm feeling quite tired so will probably call it a night.'

'Understood,' he replies. 'You do look extremely tired.'

'Thanks,' you say.

Saying you're tired is one of the most common everyday lies. As a rule it's a sign that you're bored, off-colour, having a bad time, lonely, depressed or too sober to enjoy yourself. Rarely, if ever, does it denote weariness.

You're appearing on *Love Your Garden with Alan Titchmarsh* to promote your herbaceous borders, which look stunning at this time of year. You've never done this before and have a history of behaving in a peculiar fashion when nervous, though are reluctant to admit it.

'Welcome!' says Alan.

'Thanks,' you reply. 'I just want to say upfront that I'm quite tired so if I say anything odd that'll be why.'

'No problem,' says Alan. 'So tell us about your garden.'

'YOU'RE ALL MAD AND I WANT TO BE EATEN ALIVE BY A FOX,' you scream.

'For those watching in black and white I should probably point out that you do look quite tired,' says Alan.

'Thanks,' you say.

It is impossible to challenge someone over their state of fatigue. Who are we to judge how tired a person is? It's akin to guessing their state of mind or estimating how

much cash they've got in the attic. This is why the following exchange is such a rarity:

'Sorry I'm leaving early but I'm really pooped.'
'No, you're not, you've been eating well and resting up, and I happen to know you had eleven hours sleep last night.'
'You're right, I'll stay for an extra six hours.'

The most common use of the 'tired' pretext is in situations of sexual proximity. Since human beings are biologically programmed to copulate at the drop of a hat, the suggestion of exhaustion is inevitably a device for avoidance.

'Shall we kiss and cuddle in the nude with a view to sexual intercourse?'
'Not tonight darling,' says the husband. 'I'm too tired.'
'That's not like you,' she counters.
'I know,' he says. 'The truth of the matter is I'm having an affair with Daphne from number twelve so I'm not really up for it. Maybe tomorrow?'
'We'll see. Sleep well.'
'You too.'

LIE # 98

66 Trust me. 99

'I'm scared,' you say. 'This pathway is really narrow and there's a sheer drop to the left. Plus the gravel is slippery.'

'Trust me,' comes the reply. 'I've walked this route many times in my life, often in the dark. There's nothing to be afrai—'

The phrase 'trust me' has a long and chequered past, from Neville Chamberlain to Kevin Keegan. Research suggests that 'trust me' are the world's most famous last words, along with 'does this window open?', 'cutting the red wire now' and 'we come in peace'.

'We're completely lost!' says Susan. 'Please let's stop and ask someone!'

'Trust me,' replies Rupert. 'I know where we're going.'

'You keep saying that but we've already driven into the sea and hit a nun.'

'Do you trust me?'

'Yes bu—'

'Well then.'

In professional terms, doctors are deemed the most trustworthy, although God knows they made a mess of Arthur's hip. Thanks to famous U-turns such as 'read my

lips: no more taxes' and 'honestly I promise I never slept with that flamingo', politicians reside at the bottom of the list. Estate agents are just above politicians, alongside tabloid journalists and owls (never trust an owl).

When someone requests that we trust them there is usually a degree of jeopardy involved, either personal safety or emotional well-being. The person is asking us to put our lives, our well-being – in the case of a doctor, even our intestines – in their hands. We do not enjoy this because the only person we truly trust is ourselves.

> 'This is an exercise in trust,' says the lady on the trust course. 'I want you to fall backwards into my arms.'
>
> 'You said I'd fall backwards into your arms!' you exclaim, rubbing the back of your head.
>
> 'It's important to learn that in life many people are untrustworthy.'

Just because someone claims to be an expert in their field doesn't mean we should trust them. They could be a policeman, a pilot, even a circus performer – but if they've had a bad night we're better off going with our own instincts. For instance: 'Sorry, but whatever you say my gut's telling me not to put my head in that lion's mouth.'

Most humans are trustworthy. Unfortunately, a handful are bluffing, on the make or out to impress. For such people 'trust me' is lie-speak for 'I'm desperate to get you on my side'. They are not authorities on anything, merely chancers seeking love and allies. A couple more examples:

'Go in, ask for the bladdy maney, if they don't give it get the gun out, take the bladdy maney, out again, in the car, bosh, can't fail, trust me.'

'3.15 from Chepstow. Gloomy Newsreader 66/1. Put a monkey on. I knew its father, can't lose.'

In the end trust comes down to how often someone is correct. Keep a record of decisions taken by friends and family, tot these up at the end of the year and trust the winner implicitly. Unless they're an owl.

LIE # 99

"There are a hundred lies in the *Would I Lie To You?* book."

The eagle-eyed amongst you may have already spotted this lie; after all, we did come clean on the cover of this very book. The rest of you are no doubt feeling cheated and disappointed. But look, you've had ninety-nine moments of fun. More if you count the chats with Rob, Lee and David in between the lies. Actually, thinking about it, you've only had ninety-eight, because this ninety-ninth entry isn't really a proper thing. It's just a pathetic admission that this book has failed to deliver what it promised on the cover.

What can we say? We are sorry if we've let you down.

On the upside, you've finished the book now. And isn't that a great feeling? Don't you feel intellectually nourished having spent time in the company of such brilliant minds? You are a wiser person now. You're more socially aware. From now on, you'll know when someone is lying to you. More importantly, you now have the tools to lie to others without getting caught. Think how powerful that makes you. You are invincible. You are practically a god. No, forget that. You *are* a god. There is nothing you can't

338

do. Go out into the world and shape it in your image. And when you're done with that, pop back to the shops and pick up a copy of whatever the next book from the *Would I Lie To You?* stable happens to be.

If you are still feeling aggrieved at missing the last lie, then there is a way to get one more. Walk over to the mirror and study your reflection. Stand completely still and keep looking. Look deep into the eyes of the person in the glass until they appear to be somebody else altogether. There, that's it. A stranger stands before you. Now, look this stranger in the eye and tell them the worst thing you have ever done. Don't be coy, only the two of you are in the room. Look deep into your soul and speak aloud the worst thing you have ever, ever done. Go on; be brave. On the count of three just say it. Ready?

One, two, three.

And there's the 100th lie.

You've definitely done something much worse than that.